A History of International Civil Aviation

For civil aviation to progress it has never been just about technology and business practices. To go from the rudiments of the early services that plied across short distances in Europe and America to what we experience today required most of all that politicians and policymakers address the central problems of national sovereignty over airspace and national ownership and control over airlines. Those problems have plagued the development of seamless and efficient air services for consumers in the international sphere. One would have thought that international airlines might have led the way towards a uniform globalized system given the nature of their enterprise, but that has definitely not been the case. Sovereignty and security issues have more often than not trumped commercial arguments for a more level playing field for international airlines. There has thus been an ongoing tussle between sovereignty, state security and mercantilist practices on the one hand and the ambition for civil aviation to flourish on the other. As one early commentator put it: 'one is convinced that the sovereign state cannot be left without authority over what happens just above its territory, [but] . . . one shrinks from the idea that aerial navigation could be the object of narrow-minded restrictions.' How those narrow-minded restrictions were gradually eroded, though still not eliminated, to enable civil aviation to flourish is at the heart of this work.

This book will be of direct interest to students of aviation, modern history, international relations and transport. It is also of value to airline industry professionals and government transport departments.

Alan Dobson, honorary Professor at Swansea University, has written extensively on Anglo-American relations and civil aviation. He has held fellowships at the Norwegian Nobel Institute, at St Bonaventure University (Lenna) and at Baylor University (Fulbright). He is editor of the *Journal of Transatlantic Studies* and of the *International History Review*.

A History of International Civil Aviation

From its Origins through Transformative Evolution

Alan Dobson

Routledge
Taylor & Francis Group

LONDON AND NEW YORK

First published 2017 by Routledge

2 Park Square, Milton Park, Abingdon, Oxfordshire OX14 4RN
52 Vanderbilt Avenue, New York, NY 10017

Routledge is an imprint of the Taylor & Francis Group, an informa business

First issued in paperback 2019

British Library Cataloguing-in-Publication Data
A catalogue record for this book is available from the British Library

Library of Congress Cataloging-in-Publication Data
A catalog record has been requested for this book

ISBN: 978-1-138-74559-9 (hbk)
ISBN: 978-0-367-88740-7 (pbk)

Typeset in Times New Roman
by Apex CoVantage, LLC

This is dedicated to Mya, who brings joy to our whole family and who is all set to be a high flyer.

Contents

Foreword

In 2007 in the preface to my book on the single European aviation market's origins and development, *Globalization and Regional Integration* (London: Routledge, 2007), I announced 'this will almost certainly be my last full-length study of the politics and diplomacy of international airline policy making.' One very kind response to that came from a reviewer in 2009, who said 'we can only urge Dobson to reconsider, and to compose a fourth book on aviation.' Well I did. The addiction was too strong and in 2011 *FDR and Civil Aviation* appeared (New York and London: Palgrave Macmillan 2011) and now in 2017 comes this. It is the accumulated knowledge of civil aviation spread over more than three decades and is a most appropriate way to draw my life-long study of aviation to a close, or perhaps I ought to say a near closure just in case something else were to come along.

For me one of the interesting aspects of the book is how my views and what I have to say have changed over the years in response to further archival research, interviews and analytical reflection. As my doctoral supervisor Charles Reynolds might have said and probably did say: 'All good history is revisionist history.' What follows is an explanation of how airlines operated from their infancy to the present. It is an explanation that has been honed over many years and draws out a sort of pattern of development driven by technology, business ambitions, political and security requirements and international bilateral and multilateral agreements. And all is set within the context of friction between the demands of national air sovereignty – with all that that implies – and the demands from airline businesses and consumers for more, cheaper, safer and better air travel.

I wrote this book primarily because I felt the need to do so, but it was also prompted by a constellation of factors that if I were to set down here in print would not be believed. Readers would think that I'd made it up (those who know me well know of what I speak). Whatever, the main thing is that the book is done and ready to be read and I hope that many do. It reveals a fascinating story of commercial, national security and political struggles, from which nevertheless emerged an amazingly successful industry. An industry of which millions upon millions have now had first-hand experience, but they remain largely woefully uninformed of just how they have been enabled to get from A to B with such economy, efficiency, safety and ease. Surely that is a story worth knowing.

Alan P. Dobson
November 2016

Abbreviations

AA	American Airlines
AEA	Association of European Airlines
ASA	air service agreement
ASEAN	Association of South East Asian Nations
ATC	air traffic control
ATM	air traffic management
BA	British Airways
BM	British Midland
BOAC	British Overseas Airways Corporation
CAA	(UK) Civil Aviation Authority
CAB	(US) Civil Aeronautics Board
COREPER	(EC/EU Council) Committee of Permanent Representatives
CRAF	(US) Civil Reserve Air Fleet
Cmd	(British Government) Command Paper
CRSs	computer reservation systems
CTP	Common Transport Policy
DG	(European Commission) Directorate General
EASA	European Aviation Safety Agency
EATCHIP	European Air Traffic Control Harmonization and Integration Programme
EC	European Community
ECAC	European Civil Aviation Conference
EEA	European Economic Area
EU	European Union
FABS	functional airspace blocs
HLC	High-Level Group
IATA	International Air Traffic Association
IATA	International Air Transport Association
ICAN	International Commission of Air Navigation
ICAO	International Civil Aviation Organization
ILS	instrument landing system
IMF	International Monetary Fund
IR	International regimes
IR	International relations

KLM	*Koninklijke Luchtvaart Maatschappij*
NGO	non-governmental organization
NPRM	notice of proposed rule-making
NOTAMs	Notices to Airmen
OAA	open aviation area
OPEC	Organization of Petroleum Exporting Countries
Pan Am	Pan American World Airways
PICAO	Provisional International Civil Aviation Organization
RAF	Royal Air Force
RFC	Royal Flying Corps
SAM	Single Air Market
SARPs	standards and recommended practices
SCO	Show Cause Order
SEAM	Single European Aviation Market
SES	Single European Sky
SESAME	SES Implementation Programme
TDRs	Traffic Distribution Rules
TWA	Trans World Airlines
UA	United Airlines
UAE	United Arab Emirates
UK	United Kingdom
UN	United Nations
UNDP	United Nations Development Programme
USA	United States of America
UTA	*Union de Transport Aérien*
WTO	World Trade Organization

1 Introduction

From civil aviation's origins to the Paris Convention 1919

First, one is convinced that the sovereign state cannot be left without authority over what happens just above its territory, secondly one shrinks from the idea that aerial navigation could be the object of narrow-minded restrictions.

Johana F. Lycklama á Nijeholt, 1910[1]

Introduction: the focus and the challenge

The ambition here is easy to state, less easy to deliver. The objective is to explain the development of international civil aviation from its origins in the early twentieth century to the present. From the time when there were no passenger services, and obviously no infrastructure to support them, to the present with the sleek comfort, safety and timely efficiency of the A380 with its range just short of 10,000 miles, maximum capacity of 853 passengers and cruising speed of 560 miles per hour.[2] Delivering that explanation is, however, fraught with difficulties because it is not just a story of technical advances. Planes cannot fly internationally without states granting them permission via air services agreements (ASAs) and such permission has always been accompanied by conditions. Among other things this created the central and fundamental problem for international civil aviation: tension between national sovereignty over airspace on the one hand and a growing need to avoid 'narrow-minded restrictions' on the other in order to allow international civil aviation to flourish. It is explaining the interplay between these two requirements that makes the story so difficult to tell. It will take the following six stages to accomplish:

1   From civil aviation's origins to the Paris Convention 1919
2   The inter-war predatory bilateral system 1919–1939
3   Wartime planning and the Chicago Conference 1939–1944
4   The Chicago-Bermuda regime: – creation and operation and the challenge of deregulation 1945–1992
5   The European sub-system and the creation of the Single European Aviation Market (SEAM) 1987–1997
6   Open-skies and a fully globalized world market – challenge and reality 1992–2015

The end result will be a narrative that effectively tells two stories about international aviation. The first explains a growing level of governance and uniformity of operation in the industry in the technical, infrastructure, safety, security, air traffic control and navigational spheres. These sectors are very important because of their forms of governance, which have evolved over time and because they are essential prerequisites for a successful international airline system. As a story it has its complexities, but is relatively straightforward compared to the second. It deals with the commercial operation of the airline industry, which has been dominated by national politics for reasons that will be explained more fully shortly. The consequences have been a series of operational scenarios, which cannot strictly be described as successive regimes or systems of airline operation because they have always been too fragmented and vary from one bilateral or regional aviation agreement to another. Furthermore, in the commercial sector, the controlling element has always been political (namely, the national interest of the state) and it is that which has always compromised the possibility of developing a uniform commercial operating system for international civil aviation. Those statements applied in an almost unqualified way until the 1990s when something different began to happen, with forms of commercial multilateralism holding out the possibility of a more uniform and commercially rational *modus operandi* emerging. The trajectory towards that still incompletely consummated possibility is one of the main themes of this work.

A truly uniform or what we might call a globalized international civil aviation industry has not yet emerged, but that has been the recent trajectory. Globalization here does not mean a worldwide deregulated free market. It is doubtful if that were ever possible given the nature of the beast: the safety and public service requirements; airlines as symbols and promoters of national interest; and national security benefits through up-lift capacity and civil aviation's implications for aerospace manufacturing, research and development. Even so these factors do not deny the possibility of some form of effective globalization. It would not be the same as other industries, but would have some of the same essentials: globally harmonized rules for competition, investment, ownership, safety, security and technical standards. The key to understanding the 'globalized international civil aviation market' as it is used here is the idea of a worldwide level playing field. In principle this could be run on any kind of basis, including one far from the ideal of a free and competitive market. The only overriding principle is that all players act in accordance with the same rules and regulations.

But, before examining the six successive regimes and the progress that they have made towards globalization, I suppose one might ask, why is this of interest?

Humanity's romance with the air has surely been forever, but the first practical development was the kite, used by the Chinese about 2,600 years ago. It took a long time – over 2,000 years – to move from kites to hot air balloons, but then the pace of development accelerated at a bewildering speed. From hot air balloons to powered and controlled heavier-than-air flight took 194 years and from that to 'achieving the goal . . . of landing a man on the moon and returning him safely to the earth', 66 years.[3] The twentieth and twenty-first centuries are the centuries of human flight. Such a claim needs little justification given the importance of aviation in both war and peace. If Britain had not won the Battle of Britain in 1940 it is difficult to see how a second front could ever have been launched against Hitler's fortress Europe. And after World War Two, strategic thinking became dominated in turn by the nuclear capability of long-range bombers and missiles. These facts are well known and well integrated into our understanding of the world. What is often not so well appreciated is the huge impact of civil aviation.

By 2013 airlines of two countries – the USA and China – carried over a billion domestic and international passengers and the airlines of three others over 100 million passengers each: the USA's carried a staggering 740 million; China's 352 million; the UK's 118 million; Japan's 105 million; and Germany's 105 million.[4] Such passengers were carried with impressive safety. For International Air Transport Association (IATA) member airlines – the overwhelming majority of the world's scheduled carriers – the annual accident rate per million passengers carried between 2009–2013 was by region: North Asia, 0.85; North America, 1.38; Europe: 2.03; Commonwealth of Independent States, 6.02; Middle East and North Africa, 5.76; and Africa, 13.53 (top and bottom three safety regions).[5] These things were only possible because of advancements in technology, a market of potential travelers, the adoption of uniform technical and safety standards, the gradual emergence of an international infrastructure and a myriad of international bilateral and more recently multilateral commercial agreements. The above figures speak for themselves and demonstrate the importance of both civil aviation and explaining how it got from nowhere to where we are today.

To acquire a glimpse of how all this came about, the complexities involved and how far and how swiftly aviation has moved, one only has to look at problems 80 years ago in trying to establish transatlantic air services.

In a set of complicated hybrid negotiations in 1936, American and British officials and representatives of Pan American World Airways (Pan Am) and Imperial Airways struck agreement for two round-trip transatlantic flights a week for each airline between the US and the UK. That agreement still applied in 1945 at the end of the Second World War when the Lockheed Constellation was the state of the art and available, at least for US airlines; British airlines initially had to make do with converted wartime bombers with much less capacity. The Constellation could carry roughly between 60 to 90 passengers depending on the version of the aircraft and the seat configuration. Simple mathematics tells us that amounts to a possible maximum of 360 passengers a week or 18,720 a year for travel between the US and the UK. In 2010 British Airways *alone* was flying over 65,000 seats *a week* to the US and by 2013 over 17 million passengers passed between the two countries.[6]

How that huge transformation of the airline industry happened will take some time to explain, but an immediate question is: Why were the US and Britain, the two leading aviation powers in the world, so restricted in their operations in 1945 when the following conditions applied?[7]

- Technologically it was possible in 1945 to expand civil aviation into becoming a global carrier for a mass market: the industry had the airlines, the war had seen navigational aids develop to produce a worldwide route system, and many countries had appropriate landing and take-off facilities, often courtesy of the US Army Air Force (which had succeeded the US Army Air Corps in 1941).

- The promise of opening the skies and standardization of safety and technical matters and provision of essential data meant it was possible. These were provided for at the International Civil Aviation Conference in Chicago in 1944 via the Air Transit Agreement composed of Freedoms of the Air 1 and 2 for transit and technical stop and the creation of the (Provisional) International Civil Aviation Organization (ICAO).
- Provisions for interlining and pricing through the operation of the International Air Transport Association (IATA) meant it was possible. IATA was created in 1945 by the world's major scheduled airlines.
- In terms of existing airlines in 1945, in principle, it was possible to expand civil aviation into becoming a global carrier for a mass market: US airlines such as Pan Am, American Overseas Airlines and Trans World Airlines had gained huge experience in flying transoceanic routes during the war and had safe, reliable modern passenger aircraft.
- In terms of a potential consumer market it was possible to expand civil aviation into becoming a global carrier for a mass market: falling costs, larger airlines, and increasing affluence, especially in the US, potentially offered large demand.

So why were the US and the UK restricted to two transatlantic round trips each a week? The simple answer is politics and its failure to establish a multilateral commercial aviation agreement at the International Civil Aviation Conference convened in Chicago in 1944. Politics was all: a myriad of consequences flow from that and they need to be teased out at considerable length. That will be begun shortly, but first a brief diversion into methodology and the assumptions underpinning the explanation that is to come.

Methodological interlude*

International civil aviation, like other aspects of international relations (IR), is highly complex. As a result, there have been various attempts to reduce it to its key components and dynamics for ease of explanation. In simple language, this means the generation of models or types of theory that allow us to grasp international civil aviation as a subset of IR in general. As in most cases of IR scholarship, explanation and meaning are driven by a practical agenda for improving the management of, or even transforming, relationships.[8] IR scholarship has its origins in the early twentieth century and the aftermath of World War One and the understandable desire to control or eliminate war: those motives abide. They are clearly commendable and need to be pursued robustly, but the question to be addressed briefly here is: From what are these IR theories and models constructed? They are clearly reductionist, but reductions from what?

IR literature concerned with aviation is sparse, but what there is has been largely derived from theoretical ideas that were generated in the 1970s and 1980s, resulting in what is called regime theory. This has developed over time, though not often applied to civil aviation, and is a subject of a contentious debate between scholars with affinities with the two broad schools of thought that have histori-cally lain at the center of IR scholarship: Realism and Idealism.[9] In manifestations of regime theory in the 1980s and 1990s, Realists and interdependence theorists (Idealists) argued vigorously, reflecting that age-old division and positions on a sliding scale between them. International relations operate in what Realist theo-rists call a state of anarchy, namely in a realm where there is no Leviathan to impose order and enforce the rule of law. Everything is dominated by power rela-tionships shifting and balancing over time. Today's friend may be tomorrow's enemy and there is no such thing as a defensive weapon. The world is locked into a security dilemma where one state's security through the accumulation of military power (defensive weapons) is seen by others as the power to aggress (offensive weapons) and so arms' races begin. Idealists in contrast emphasize the importance of international law and custom, mutual benefits from trade and the ability of rational discourse through diplomacy to transcend suspicions and build bonds of trust. While acknowledging the pervasiveness of international power politics, they also see an international society running in parallel, which enables the formation and efficient operation of activities, organizations and regimes such as the United Nations (UN), the International Monetary Fund (IMF), the World Trade Organization (WTO), aid and development non-governmental organi-zations (NGOs) and civil aviation, all of which cut across and help to temper and restrict power relationships.[10] Notwithstanding these different theoretical approaches, how regimes emerge and develop are important questions for both schools of thought, though as we might suspect they answer them in radically different ways. How can 'islands of order . . . form in an ocean of disorder'? How can 'patterns of rule-guided policy coordination emerge, maintain themselves, and decay [or thrive and develop]' in the international system?[11]

Something strange is happening here with some measure of agreement, but then radical disagreements between contending schools of thought. As one Realist scholar puts it:

> The position of all regime theorists, regardless of whether they are insti-tutionalists or modified structural realists, can be translated into a single hypothesis: Given the considerable interdependence in the world, IRs [inter-national regimes] are pervasive in the international system – particularly in issue-areas that lie outside the zero-sum realm of security – and, once they are created are likely to persist.[12]

So, there is some agreement about the overall architecture of international regimes; however, after that these two theoretical approaches yield radically dif-ferent results.

For Realists, international regimes, such as the aviation system, are epiphe-nomena, which reflect arrangements that suit the dominant power or powers: they have no life or self-sustaining potential of their own. In the words of Baldev Raj Nayar, who has interrogated the nature of international civil aviation, power is *the* explanatory variable. States behave 'as a function of shifts in the balance of power; accordingly, as the balance of power changes, so does the regime.' The civil aviation regime, like any other has been 'driven by power and state interests, rather than commitment to shared values and norms or enthusiasm for the provision of collective goods.' As Nayar has also noted:

> Even regimes that seem to have been negotiated may be so only in form; they may actually have been imposed if negotiated in the shadow of preponderant power, with their articulated principles or norms serving as an ideological mask for domination, as in the case of nuclear nonproliferation or missile technology control.[13]

In order to assess:

> The question of whether IR (international regime) norms in aviation are a reflection of or a constraint on the balance of power or both requires that the examination encompasses a considerable stretch of historical time, rather than a single bargaining episode.[14]

In other words to assess his claims about the explanatory efficacy of his preferred theory compared with Liberal Institutionalists, Nayar turns to history.

In sharp contrast to this Realist view, Christer Jönsson, drawing heavily on the work of Robert Keohane and Joseph Nye,[15] believes that international regimes might best be thought of as 'intermediary normative frameworks which facilitate the making of substantial agreements in a given issue area' and, once created, develop lives and bureaucratic mores of their own, which persist and develop over time to become significant transnational players in their own right in their respective issue areas.[16] Having committed himself to the existence of international regimes of a specific character, and one different from the Realists, Jönsson then goes on to identify ways in which regime creation and development can be explained. He does this by a lengthy analysis invoking four models of explanation, which he deems to be mutually supportive. In this he is following in the footsteps of Graham Allison.[17] Jönsson's four cuts at explanation are: economic, divided into technology and supply and demand issues; political structural, looking at the shifts in power relations; situational, meaning what types of situations trigger the creation and revision of regimes; and finally a process model, which draws on bargaining theory and inter-organization theory. To evaluate the explanatory strengths of these models and how one might apply more than another in specific instances, Jönsson then turns to historical case studies to assess them.[18]

In short, both Nayar and Jönsson, aware that their results are contentious, turn to the historical record to bolster the strength and accuracy of their respective approach. However, part of the problem here is that their conceptual frameworks prioritize and select 'historical evidence', compressing it into partly preconceived patterns rather than allowing the explanation to be evidence driven. One observation about that would be that these IR theory approaches in fact do not yield explanation as such – the generation of knowledge for its own sake – but are a form of practical explanation for achieving practical results. They are conceptualizations/reductions of existing knowledge with the intent that such knowledge be used effectively in the world of practice.[19] If this is correct, and the present author does subscribe to this view, then the key thing is to get the knowledge-for-its-own-sake explanation right first, and here that is taken to be historical explanation, for only then can accurate conceptualization and model building for effective practical action be accomplished. Put another way, the answer to the question posed above is that reduction in both cases is from history. At times the explanation that follows here is truncated or abbreviated through the use of footnote references to more detailed evidence to support the explanation. This is for the sake of brevity, flow and lucidity, but hopefully without losing the integrity of an historical explanatory narrative.

From the Wright brothers to the Paris Convention 1919

In the beginning there were lawyers and discussion of theoretical possibilities. As early as 1880 at their conference in Oxford, the private association of jurists, who made up the *Instut de Droit International* (Institute of International Law), discussed aviation matters. These people were important for exploring issues connected with the potential for international aviation, both civil and military. As one expert on air law has put it: 'As early as 1900, the French jurist Fauchille suggested that a code of international air navigation be created by the '*Instut de Droit International*'. Interestingly, this was one of the rare instances where legal process went ahead of technology.'[20] Jönsson believes that the views its members expressed were for a while the dominant voice in international aviation. They looked towards a kind of freedom of the air for aviation and he argues that it was not until World War One and the establishment of transnational groups of military personnel and war bureaucrats that there was a radical change of direction towards national sovereignty over airspace.

> World War 1 drastically changed the context of bargaining. Not only did it tip the balance between legal and military considerations, but it also entailed the establishment of new transnational networks, which were ultimately far more influential than the early network of jurists.[21]

Obviously, World War One had huge impact on everything that came after, but the balance on civil aviation was tipped *before* 1914 and that tipping was not as dramatic as Jönsson suggests because the debate was not as sharply polarized as he portrays. Neither Fauchille nor his main opponent John Westlake, a leading British jurist, were purist proponents respectively of air freedom and national air sovereignty. Furthermore, in the ongoing debate that began at the start of the twentieth century, those who inclined to a more permissive regime were already under pressure before World War One. And finally, German and French jurists, who had argued for a form of open skies, had already signed up to national sovereignty over airspace before the war and for its part Britain had always espoused such a position. What we can say is that between the First International Congress of Aeronautics attended by Brazil, France, the UK, the USA, Mexico and Russia at the time of the Paris International Exhibition in 1889 and the Ghent meeting of the Institute of International Law in 1906, the freedom of the air doctrine developed by Paul Fauchille held center stage. However, it is important to note that for much of this time it was all rather academic and hypothetical. But, by 1906 matters were beginning to change: Aviation would soon have more practical consequences and when Fauchille pushed for a code of laws to regulate aerial navigation in peacetime and in war along permissive lines, John Westlake took issue with him.

Although Westlake objected to Fauchille's approach, his counterproposal at Ghent did not embody the principle of absolute national air sovereignty:

> The state has a right of sovereignty over aerial space above its soil, saving a right of inoffensive passage (usage) for balloons and other aerial machines and for communication by wireless telegraphy.[22]

Westlake's views were in a distinct minority at Ghent, but the debate between him and Fauchille dominated subsequent meetings of the Institute and gradually Westlake's views began to recruit support. One must add that the challenge facing Westlake was not quite so daunting as it might first appear. The view from most countries was not homogeneous and even in France, which initially championed a form of freedom of the air, there were powerful dissenting voices, most notably from the military. The result of all this was that in 1910, when Fauchille presented a code of air law at the International Air Navigation Conference in Paris, 18 May to 29 June, French and German delegates argued for a form of Grotius's *mare liberum* applied to the air, but they were opposed, most notably, by the British, and, as a result, final agreement eluded the delegates. This was, specifically, because of articles 19 and 20 'dealing with restrictions which states might impose on foreign aircraft in the air space above its territory.'[23] As an authoritative legal text puts it: 'Contrary to general assumption, this Conference did not adopt the "freedom of the air" theory. At that time the general tendency was already in favor of the principle of the sovereignty of States in the space above their territories.'[24] Westlake's views were clearly gaining ground. In the Anglo-Saxon world of Britain and the US they were already well embedded and partly because of doctrine drawn from Common Law:

> Under principles of Anglo-American common law, the owner of land also owned the space above the land, with no height limit. As the ancient maxim put it, *cujus est solum ejus usque ad coelum* – he who owns the soil owns up to the sky.[25]

This principle mattered because Britain and the US would soon become leaders in international civil aviation.

By the time of the Madrid meeting in 1911 things had developed into a rather endearing ambiguity.

> In conclusion of the International Law Association at its meeting in Madrid in 1911, the most widely held opinions among the jurists were expressed thus:
>
> 1   States have the right to regulate traffic over their territory (land and sea).
> 2   While reserving this right they should permit free transit to airships of all nations.[26]

A state's security, however, cannot live by ambiguity and that same year the British government passed the Aerial Navigation Act, which maintained that the air over Britain, its Empire and Dominions was inviolable. The Home Secretary was allocated the power of control, but interestingly in 1913 when the Act was amended the authority was transferred to the Secretary for War – a move charged with all kinds of implications for the future. In 1913 France and Germany signed the first international aviation treaty and followed suit in that: 'sovereignty of the state over its airspace was maintained.'[27] Even the Institute of International Law seemed to land on Westlake's side when it adopted the following resolution:

> It is the right of every State to enact such prohibitions, restrictions and regulations as it may think proper in regard of the passage of aircraft above its territories and territorial waters. Subject to this right of subjacent States, liberty of passenger aircraft ought to be accorded freely to the aircraft of every nation.[28]

Much hinges here on the force of the word *ought*: if it is not compelling then we have the dominance of state sovereignty over national airspace; if it is, then this opens the way for qualified national air sovereignty. But given what Germany and France did in the first international aviation treaty, one could be tempted to say that if sovereignty over national airspace were not dominant it was certainly rapidly gaining ascendancy. There was little ground to travel from this position of principle to outright sovereignty over airspace asserted by the Paris Convention in 1919: but there was a huge expanse of ground to cover in terms of substantive international law. Apart from the bilateral treaty between France and Germany, international air law could hardly be said to exist. At the Second Hague Peace Conference in 1907, the delegates had agreed to 'prohibit for a period extending to the close of the Third Peace Conference, the discharge of projectiles and explosives from balloons or by other new methods of similar nature.'[29] Over twenty states signed the declaration, but significant countries such as Germany, Italy, Japan and Russia did not and so it could not be 'regarded as an integral part of international law.' There was not sufficient consensus for international law to come into being.[30] When the delegations assembled in Paris in 1918 formally to end the war and structure the future peace they were thus confronted with a virtual blank slate in terms of the substance of international law and regulation for governing civil aviation.

In August 1914 when British Foreign Secretary Sir Edward Grey remarked to a friend: '*The lamps are going out all over Europe, we shall not see them lit again in our life-time*', he spoke truer than he knew. Change was upon Europe in a way never experienced before and its impact was ubiquitous. Civil aviation was not and could not be left untouched and so with war came the closing of national airspace in Europe and the vision of H.G. Wells in his best-seller *The War in the Air* written in 1907 and first published in 1908 was realized. As one of his characters put it speaking of military planes: 'I don't mean flap up and smash up; I mean real, safe, steady, controlled flying, against the wind, good and right.' Such machines created a reality more brutal and intimidating than even the master of science-fiction fantasy had imagined.[31] The debate about national sovereignty over airspace could not remain unmoved by these developments. Already leaning strongly to its adoption, now, and for a seemingly interminably long time to come, the international consensus committed to sovereignty over national airspace. But as we have seen already, this was never really conceived of as a simple either-or-choice between absolute sovereignty and freedom of the skies. The debate between Fauchille and Westlake reflected different and strong inclinations, but neither were purists. What the 1914–1918 war did was to push consensus even further towards the purist sovereignty position, though as will be seen it never fully arrived there.

The British position at the end of the war was bound to be influential because it was the greatest-ever empire covering vast swathes of the world; it was one of the victors; and with 27,000 officers and 260,000 other ranks in the Royal Air Force (RAF),[32] 23,000 aircraft and 700 aerodromes, it was the leading air power. As early as May 1917 the government in London began to think about post-war aviation and appointed a Civil Air Transport Committee to consider matters and make recommendations. The committee, briefly chaired by the newspaper baron Lord Northcliffe, soon passed to Major J.L. Baird, the Undersecretary of State for Air. It was tasked with considering:

> the steps which should be taken with a view to the development and regulation after the War of aviation for civil and commercial purposes from a domestic, an imperial and an international standpoint.[33]

Its key recommendation in December 1918 when it reported was: 'We think that the claim to full and absolute sovereignty should be emphasized in the preamble to the Bill.'[34] That was the overall position adopted by the British in Paris, but with important caveats.

When the delegates assembled to craft the peace settlement it did not take long to establish the Aeronautical Commission of the Peace Conference. In effect it was the Inter-allied Aviation Committee set up in September 1917 to coordinate allied air power under a new name. This may, as Jönsson suggests, have been one of the reasons why swift progress was made towards the emergence of the Paris Convention, but this pre-existing military transnational network was hardly a determining factor in the ready acceptance of national air sovereignty in Paris. The international jurist network that had taken up the issue of what to do about airspace and had advocated a liberal type of freedom of the air had already lost the argument well before the World War began. The irony at Paris was that France, which had initially been at the forefront of championing freedom of the air, now became a leading regulator. France fell among those who objected to Anglo-American arguments for qualifying national air sovereignty with liberal freedoms to enable the development of international aviation. For the British there were two main reasons for their position: the first was a fear that imperial communication lines would be made more difficult if countries were not generally committed to a liberal system of innocent passage; and the second was the prospect of commercial gain through developing British airlines for both passenger and mail delivery services. In contrast, the French, in the light of their war experience, demanded a more extensive form of air sovereignty. They were on strong ground. Common sense in the light of World War One simply confirmed what had already become the dominant commitment prior to the war, namely that there had to be air sovereignty. Also, one needs to bear in mind the infant state of the aviation passenger industry. Strictly speaking it still did not exist, and so there was little commercial vested interest to promote a liberal skies regime. Not surprisingly then, the French position prevailed.[35] So often in the development of aviation it has been necessary to accept the lowest common denominator for policy developments. It is largely the nature of the enterprise that dictates this: there always have to be willing players for airlines to operate internationally; no state can do it alone.

The Convention Relating to the Regulation of Aerial Navigation signed at Paris, October 13, 1919 (The Paris Convention) at first glance seems forthright and crystal clear. Article 1 declared: 'The High Contracting Parties recognize that every Power has complete and exclusive sovereignty over the air space above its territory.' The Convention then immediately modified that prescription in practice by granting rights of innocent passage to planes of Member States without discrimination, but this did not create a framework for commercial civil aviation. The key article so far as that was concerned was 15, which stated: 'The establishment of international airways shall be subject to the consent of the States flown over.'[36] In other words routes, landing rights, and all other commercial aspects of air travel were open to negotiation. At the same time it was clear in the Convention that it was expected that commercial rights would be granted. The preamble to the Convention specified as one of its motives the desire 'to encourage the peaceful intercourse of nations by means of aerial communications' and furthermore it also sought some form of uniformity in that intercourse by encouraging all nations to accede to the Convention. Non-members should only be provided with temporary *ad hoc* arrangements: 'Article 5: No contracting State shall, except by a special and temporary authorization, permit the flight above its territory of an aircraft which does not possess the nationality of a contracting State.' Much of the character of the post-war civil aviation regime would thus depend on how aviation diplomacy developed and applied the somewhat incompatible provisions of the Paris Convention.

There were other significant provisions in the convention, which set useful precedents. The Convention acknowledged the right to cabotage (retaining domestic services for a country's own airlines) and that international airlines could only take advantage of the provisions of the Convention if they were incorporated as a company with single nationality. There were also attempts to standardize aircraft registration and airworthiness, certify pilots and crew according to accepted standards, create navigational and safety provisions and standardize documentation for international flights. These technical matters were placed mainly in the hands of a new permanent body which functioned under the auspices (though in practice largely autonomously) of the League of Nations, the International Commission of Air Navigation (ICAN). Its role of trying to facilitate the growth of international aviation was soon supplemented when a handful of European airlines established the International Air Traffic Association (IATA), which looked to enable interlining, standardization of ticketing and agreements on pricing.

Conclusion

By 1919 there was little doubt that the Gordian knot tying national sovereignty to the airspace above nations had been pulled tight, but precisely what it entailed still had to be determined. Jurists had initiated the debate about what to do with airspace and their inclination, largely pushed by the energy and strength of Fauchille's arguments, had been towards a liberal regime of a kind of open-skies. How dominant such views ever became remains rather contentious, but two things are clear. Firstly, Britain, the most powerful country in the world with influence over a larger sphere than any other, was from the outset opposed to Fauchille's version of freedom of the skies and always placed more emphasis on the importance of sovereignty over airspace. Secondly, once technological developments made the vision of air travel an imminent reality, the argument shifted ineluctably away from the more liberal open sky to a more conservative sovereignty of the air position. This in turn reflected two important considerations: the first, which came to apply almost universally, was the obsession with security and fear of death raining down from the skies; the second, which applied in common law countries, was the legal principle of *cujus est solum ejus usque ad coelom*. Under these circumstances and in the aftermath of the First World War, it seems pretty inevitable that states would lean toward caution and assert sovereignty over airspace. It is also important to note that in 1919 there were virtually no international air services and hence no vested interests to argue for a more open sky regime.[37] In the end the emphasis was definitely on sovereign control, but that was in tension with needs, which would facilitate international communications through the development of airmail and passenger markets. These considerations influenced British and to a lesser extent American thinking in Paris and it was they who proposed a system that would have qualified sovereignty over airspace, but ironically it was France which now did most to oppose this and oppose it successfully. Even so, it was apparent that something more adventurous might eventually succeed a rigid form of air sovereignty and that had at least been clearly articulated in a major political international forum and vestiges remained in the Paris Convention.

In addition to the air sovereignty issue, there were subsidiary, but nevertheless significant, technical and organizational developments. Two permanent international civil aviation organizations emerged: one from the Paris Convention, ICAN; and the second from a meeting of European airline executives, which created the IATA.[38] Both organizations were specifically meant to facilitate the growth of international aviation, and they also held out the promise of an international bureaucracy emerging with vested interests in the perpetuation and growth of the industry.

Clearly the Paris Convention had ensured that there would be a large element of sovereign control over airspace, entailing rather narrow-minded restrictions. However, there was an element of ambiguity in the Paris Convention and space for diplomacy to be creative regarding the continuing tension between air sovereignty and the needs of an international aviation system; only time, chance and practice would reveal how these tensions would be resolved. Similarly how ICAN and IATA developed, or failed to develop, necessary international infrastructure and transnational bureaucracies would also only become clear with developments in the inter-war period.

Notes

* Those uninterested in methodology might painlessly skip this section.
1 Johana F. Lycklama á Nijeholt, *Air Sovereignty*, The Hague: Martinus Nijhoff, 1910, p. 10.
2 In practice the maximum number of passengers is probably around 540, even though the aircraft is certified to carry 853.
3 It is well established that the Chinese were flying kites in the fifth century BC. On 8 August 1709 Father Bartolomeu de Gusmão demonstrated a model hot air balloon before the Portuguese royal family and nobility at the Casa da India in Lisbon. Orville and Wilbur Wright piloted the first successful controlled flight of a powered heavier-than-air machine on 17 December 1903. John Kennedy made his famous commitment to a moon landing on 25 May 1961 and that commitment was duly consummated on 20 July 1969, by Neil Armstrong and Buzz Aldrin, in the landing craft The Eagle, carried to the moon by Apollo 11.
4 'Air Transport, passengers carried.' International Civil Aviation Organization, Civil Aviation Statistics of the World and ICAO staff estimates, http://data.worldbank.org/indicator/IS.AIR.PSGR, retrieved 17 December 2014.
5 IATA Safety Report 2013, http://www.iata.org/publications/Pages/wats.aspx, retrieved 17 December 2014.
6 British Government Command Paper, Cm 8584, *Aviation Policy Framework*, March 2013, p. 32.
7 UK Civil Aviation Authority Statistics, http://www.anna.aero/2011/01/19/uk-us-transatlantic-air-traffic-down-3pc-in-2010/, retrieved 15 May 2014.
8 Martin Hollis and Steve Smith, *Explaining and Understanding International Relations*, Oxford: Clarendon Press, 1991.
9 IR theory is fraught with multiple theoretical approaches, schools and sub-schools of thought; however, this largely revolves around the long-standing division between

Realist state/communitarian and power-centric conservative views of humanity and the state system on the one hand and Idealist and more optimistic, Liberal, internationalist and cosmopolitan views on the other. See for example, D.A. Baldwin, *Neorealism and Neoliberalism: The Contemporary Debate*, New York: Columbia University Press, 1993.

10 Hedley Bull, *The Anarchical Society: A Study of Order in World Politics*, New York: Columbia University Press, 1977; Stephen D. Krasner, 'Structural Causes and Regime Consequences: Regimes as Intervening Variables' and Susan Strange, 'Cave! Hic Dragones: A Critique of Regime Analysis', both in Krasner (editor), *International Regimes*, Ithaca: Cornell University Press, 1983, pp. 185–205 and pp. 337–353; Baldev Raj Nayar, 'Regimes, Power, and International Aviation', *International Organization* 49(i), (1995), pp. 139–71.

11 E.B. Haas, 'Why Collaborate? Issue-Linkage and International Regimes', *World Politics* 32, (1980), pp. 357–405, at p. 385; R.O. Keohane, *After Hegemony: Cooperation and Discord in the World Political Economy*, Princeton: Princeton University Press, 1984, p. 51.

12 Nayar, 'Regimes, Power and International Aviation', p. 143.

13 *Ibid.*, pp. 142, 169–70, 141.

14 *Ibid.*, p. 145.

15 Robert O. Keohane and Joseph S. Nye, *Power and Interdependence*, Boston: Little Brown, 1977; R.O. Keohane, *After Hegemony: Cooperation and Discord in the World Political Economy*, Princeton: Princeton University Press, 1984. Keohane's position is complex, as he has attempted to reconcile Realism and Liberalism/Idealism.

16 Christer Jönsson, *International Aviation and the Politics of Regime Change*, London: Frances Pinter, 1987, p. 13.

17 Graham T. Allison, *Essence of Decision: Explaining the Cuban Missile Crisis*, Boston: Little Brown, 1971.

18 Jönsson, *International Aviation*, chapters 5, 6 and 7.

19 Charles Reynolds, *Theory and Explanation in International Relations*, London: Martin Robertson, 1973; Michael Oakeshott, 'On the Activity of Being a Historian', in *Rationalism in Politics and Other Essays*, Indianapolis: Liberty Press, 1991, pp. 137–168.

20 I.H.Ph. Diederiks-Verschoor (revised by Pablo Mendes de Leon), *An Introduction to Air Law*, 9th edition, The Netherlands: Kluwer Law International, 2012, p. 2.

21 Jönsson, *International Aviation*, p. 83.

22 Westlake's proposal at Ghent cited from Amos S. Hershey, 'The International Law of Aerial Space', *The American Journal of International Law* 6(ii), (1912), pp. 381–8 at p. 382.

23 Sheila F. Macbrayne, 'The Right of Innocent Passage', *McGill Law Journal* I, (1954–55), pp. 271ff, at p. 272.

24 Diederiks-Verschoor, *Introduction to Air Law*, p. 3.

25 Stuart Banner, *Who Owns the Sky? The Struggle to Control Airspace from the Wright Brothers On*, Cambridge: Harvard University Press, 2008, p. 6.

26 Quoted from Gbenga Oduntan, *Sovereignty and Jurisdiction in the Airspace and Outer Space: Legal Criteria*, Abingdon: Routledge, 2012, p. 61.

27 *Ibid.*

28 *Ibid.*, p. 62.

29 Quoted from Hershey, 'International Law', p. 383; see also K.W. Colegrove, *International Control of Aviation*, Boston: World Peace Foundation, 1930.

30 Hershey, 'International Law', p. 383. There are two principal sources of international law: 'Customary international law is an informal, unwritten body of rules that derives from the practice of states together with *opinio juris* – a belief, on the part of governments, that the practice is required by law or is at least of relevance to its ongoing evolution . . . Only if most states support, and none or only a few oppose, it can the desired

new rule become a binding rule of customary law.' 'Treaties are quasi-contractual writ-ten instruments entered into by two or more states and registered with a third party, usually the UN Secretary-General.' And such laws are interpreted according to the virtually universally accepted 1969 Vienna Convention on the Law of Treaties: Article 31(i) providing that 'A treaty shall be interpreted in good faith in accordance with the ordinary meaning to be given to the terms of the treaty in their context and in the light of its object and purpose.' Quoted from Michael Byers and Simon Chesterman, 'Changing the Rules about Rules? Unilateral Humanitarian Intervention and the Future of International Law', in J.L. Holgrefe and Robert O. Keohane (editors), *Humanitarian Intervention: Ethical, Legal, and Political Dilemmas*, Cambridge: Cambridge University Press, 2003, pp. 179–80.

31 H.G. Wells, *The War in the Air*, London: Gollanz, 2011, p. 4. For the most extraordi-nary and moving account of aerial combat in World War One, see Cecil Lewis, *Sagit-tarius Rising*, Barnsley: Frontline Books, 2009, first published 1936, for some of the best fictional accounts see the early 'Biggles' stories by W.E. Johns, for example 'The White Fokker', in *The Camels Are Coming*, London: Red Fox Publishing, 2003 (first published 1932), pp. 16–17.

32 The Royal Flying Corps merged with the Royal Naval Air Service in November 1918 to become the RAF.

33 British Government Command Paper 9218, *Civil Aerial Transport Committee Report*, 12 December 1918.

34 *Ibid.*, interestingly one of the dissenters on the Committee was H.G. Wells who did not think that the report went far enough in encouraging the development of aviation.

35 John C. Cooper, 'Some Historic Phases in British International Civil Aviation Policy', *International Affairs* 23, (1947), pp. 189–202.

36 British Government Command Paper 266, *Convention Relating to International Air Transport*, 1919.

37 The first sustained international passenger service began in March 1919 between Paris and Brussels.

38 The International Air Traffic Association was later superseded by the International Air Transport Association after World War Two, both rather confusingly have the acronym IATA.

2 The inter-war predatory bilateral system 1919–1939

Neither of these Conventions (Paris and Havana) made provision for international regulation in the economic, as opposed to the technical field. In the result the growth of air transport was conditioned by political rather than economic considerations and its development as an orderly system of world communications was impeded. Summed up, the major evils of the pre-war period were, first, that any country on an international air route could hold operators of other countries to ransom even if those operators only wished to fly over or refuel in its territory; secondly, that there was no means of controlling the heavy subsidization of airlines which all too often were maintained at great cost for reasons mainly of national prestige or as a war potential; thirdly, that the bargaining for transit and commercial rights introduced extraneous considerations and gave rise to international jealousies and mistrust.

British Government Cmd. 6561, 'International Air Transport' 1944

Introduction: the focus and the challenge

Whatever promise the Paris Convention offered for the promotion of an efficient, uniform and safe international civil aviation system was compromised by the wider political context, which resulted in two tragic failures.

The first was the Versailles Treaty itself. It perpetuated long-term insecurity and economic instability, the reasons for which were captured best in John Maynard Keynes' *The Economic Consequences of the Peace*. The peace settlement was confronted by huge challenges and foundered primarily on the other-worldly idealism of US President Wilson clashing with French Prime Minister Clemenceau's bleak pessimism, love of France and determination to impose a punitive peace. Wilson had 'no plan, no scheme, no constructive ideas whatsoever for clothing with the flesh of life the commandments which he thundered from the White House.' 'There can seldom have been a statesman of first rank more incompetent than the President in the agilities of the council chamber.'[1] Furthermore, with specific reference to aviation Wilson seems to have been particularly ill equipped to deal with the pressing challenges of an industry poised to enter the international realm in a substantial way. While he established the US National Advisory Committee for Aeronautics in 1915, that would seem to represent his high tide of achievement in the field. He subsequently paid aviation scant attention and at Versailles he evinced little or no comprehension of the industry: the British had to press him even to consider it.

Concerning the larger issues at the conference, Wilson, in his dealings with prime ministers Lloyd George of Britain and Clemenceau, was a babe in the woods. The result was a configuration of economic, political and security measures that ineluctably led subsequently to bridling at the peace terms, rising tensions, economic disarray and depression and the gradual dismantling of the international system overseen by the League of Nations. The final chapter was descent into war. It was in this fraught international political system that the fledgling civil aviation industry tried to take flight.

The second problem was the failure of the US Senate to ratify the Versailles Treaty, which, among other things, meant that the US was not party to the Paris Convention. An industry that would eventually need uniform operating procedures and standards was already riven between the Americas on the one hand and Europe on the other.

Within this broad and flawed political context there were three generic challenges for civil aviation in the inter-war period: technological, commercial and political. Firstly, there were the technological challenges of producing reliable passenger planes and navigating them safely across vast continental and oceanic reaches. Secondly, there was the commercial challenge of making airlines financially sustainable. And thirdly, there were a series of political and governance challenges that linked with every part of the business: How could transit, technical stop and commercial rights be secured and who should negotiate for them, governments or individual airlines? Should they be granted only on a bilateral or on some form of multilateral basis? How were air routes to be provided with navigational facilities and who should pay for them? Who would set appropriate safety standards and operating procedures? What qualifications should apply to pilots and aircrew and who or what should award them? What kind of provisions should there be for interlining (travel involving two or more different airlines) and international ticketing and the fair allocation and distribution of revenue when more than one airline was involved?

To some ears these questions may seem an over-exaggeration of the problems, but they are not. The aviation industry was in its infancy. It had emerged simultaneously in several advanced industrial countries and grown haphazardly with little regulation or control. While private flying remained confined within national borders this was not a great issue, but as mail and passenger services began to develop the problem of public safety emerged and governments then made decisions about what rules and regulations might be appropriate. That very factor, the creation of a mosaic of different national rules, in turn became a problem once international flying became commonplace because there was no person or any organization in a position to create uniformity by supplanting national with international standards. The first airmail service was in the US between New York and Washington, DC, begun on 15 May 1918 and the first sustained regular domestic and international passenger services were respectively between Berlin and Weimar starting in February 1919 and between Paris and Brussels starting in March 1919. Technology was thus creating political and governance challenges, many of the most basic kind. As one historian aptly put it:

> It may sound very elementary now, but it was then necessary to make a recommendation to the effect that throttle controls on all aircraft should be so arranged that a push forward meant acceleration and push back meant closing down. The same kind of apparently elementary recommendations were needed in almost all technical matters, including such things as fuel intakes, other aircraft instrumentation and controls etc.[2]

Clearly, civil aviation faced daunting challenges in the inter-war period. The attempt of the Paris Convention to meet the desire 'to encourage the peaceful intercourse of nations by means of aerial communications' only met with meagre success. It did not create an adequate framework for the development of international civil aviation. In what follows the three challenges posed above will be examined in turn in order to assess how civil aviation progressed. Much more space will be devoted to the political and governance challenge than to the other two. In fact two sections are devoted to politics and governance: one dealing with a raft of generic issues; the second focusing on Anglo-American discussions to inaugurate transatlantic services in order to fully demonstrate the politically competitive and complex nature of inter-war bilateralism. In contrast both the technological and financial sustainability issues are treated together in the following section.

Responding to the challenges of technology and financial sustainability[3]

In the inter-war period, it was the Americans and the Germans who did most to develop domestic and regional passenger services, while the British, Dutch and again the Americans pioneered vast long-range routes. In the cases of Germany and the US there were ironies. Germany was barred for many years from developing military aircraft and so ploughed huge energy and resources into civilian airships and aircraft. As a result it became the world leader in air travel in the 1920s and by the mid-1930s Lufthansa flew twice as many passenger miles as Imperial Airways. The irony for the US was that in the immediate post-war period the land of the Wright brothers – the great pioneer of aviation – fell well behind its European counterparts.

> Up to 1927, although hundreds of thousands of Europeans had done so, practically nobody in the United States had traveled by air. In all the country there were but thirty airliners, all together holding seats for no more than two hundred passengers. Despite expectations, there had been no aviation boom in the land of the Wright brothers after World War I.[4]

There were several reasons for this but the reluctance of America's rugged form of capitalism to provide subsidies for the infant industry was one of the key ones. Elsewhere, particularly in continental Europe, there were fewer inhibitions and many airlines received substantial government subsidies. However, beginning in 1925 matters changed dramatically in the US. Between May 1927 and October 1929 nearly $1 billion flooded into the industry. By 1929 the US had overtaken Germany, the European leader in air passenger traffic. In 1930 US airlines carried more passengers than the rest of the world put together and by 1933 US airlines carried 550,000 passengers, just short of a hundred times more than barely eight years earlier.[5]

The reason for these dramatic changes was threefold. The first reason was the Kelly Airmail Act, which provided attractive and effectively subsidy-level remuneration for the carriage of mail. The second was that there were the recommendations of the Morrow Board, 1926, Chaired by Dwight Morrow, the then future father-in-law of Charles Lindberg, the first to fly solo non-stop across the Atlantic, 20–21 May 1927. The Morrow Board was spawned by a confluence of rather different but connected politically controversial developments all concerned with fears about the US lagging behind other countries in aviation. Many attributed this to the federal government's failure 'to provide machinery to encourage and regulate the use of aircraft in commerce.'[6] In particular there was growing anxiety among and criticism from members of the Army Air Service (re-titled the Army Air Corps by the 1926 Air Commerce Act). These criticisms were the most vituperative from Brigadier General William 'Billy' Mitchell. A First World War hero and leader of the American expeditionary air force in France, he was a man fully committed to the importance of air power. So, the Morrow Board was set up first and foremost to deal with the problem of America's military air power, but its recommendations did much to facilitate the growth of the civilian sector. It recommended the creation of a government regulatory department for civil aviation, the expansion of the airmail contract system, and the creation of a national system of airways, navigational infrastructure and airports with funding provided by the federal, state and municipal governments. In the main, these proposals were implemented.

This was essentially catch-up by the US. Britain, France, Holland and Germany, to name but the main countries, were already heading down this kind of road, though Britain less quickly than the others. Civil aviation was just too important to be left to the vagaries of the marketplace. Bottom line in the US after the Morrow Board report was always that American civil aviation had to flourish and if that meant subsidies then so be it. But rather characteristically of American general attitudes towards the marketplace, there was resistance to recognizing this reality. The US president at the time, Herbert Hoover, insisted that subsidies should only be a temporary measure and the Morrow Board emphasized that the infrastructure developments proposed would involve indirect and not direct subsidies of the kind, which many foreign airlines received and which were 'un-American'. Such attitudes persisted over time and disguised the extent to which civil aviation received various kinds of government support in the US.

As one scholar points out British government data indicated that subsidies via airmail contracts was twelve times higher in the US than in the UK.[7]

In Britain the need for subsidies was also becoming dramatically apparent. After holding the lead in aviation at the end of the war, Britain's position soon slipped back. Parsimonious government budgets and the prioritization of the RAF began to undermine the prospects for civil aviation. Some in government were simply ideologically ill-disposed to the idea of subsidies, but there was also the fact that aviation was largely unproved as an effective form of transport whereas rail was not and, unlike in France, the rail network in Britain was intact after the war. By 1920 British airlines were struggling to compete with their heavily subsidized French counterparts and by February 1921 British companies had ceased to operate cross-channel services. In 1922, Britain had approximately 575 military aircraft and 167 civilian compared respectively with France's 2,180 and 660. British civil aviation needed help but the government indulged in endless debate about what to do. Subsidies were introduced eventually, but it was not until the Conservatives came to power in 1922 and the appointment of Sir Samuel Hoare as Air Minister that more financial security for the industry became assured through subsidies and the mail service.[8] On 1 April 1924 another important step was taken when Imperial Airways was formed through the amalgamation of several companies: it was to receive preferential government subsidies in an attempt to create an airline capable of competing with French and other international airlines. In effect Britain had a chosen instrument for its overseas routes and Imperial Airways worked closely with the government to develop long-haul routes to connect the empire together, not least of all by the delivery of airmail.[9] The pattern in Britain for the creation of financial sustainability for the infant airline industry was the same as in the US and elsewhere: direct or indirect government subsidies and a blurring of the line between government chosen-instrument airlines for overseas operations and government in developing routes, navigational and physical infrastructure.

However, with civil aviation it is never possible to compartmentalize things too tightly. Subsidies were never simply about achieving financial sustainability for the airlines. It is true that President Hoover's justification for subsidies and huge local government expenditure on infrastructure was largely in terms of commercial pay-offs from a well-established and thriving civil aviation industry; however, he had another line of argument, which connected strongly with defense – the original motor behind the creation of the Morrow Board:

> I need not emphasize the importance of commercial aviation as an arm of defense. While it is not possible that the actual commercial plane will be much use in actual battle, yet the building up of the manufacturing industry behind such aviation is of the most vital importance. And we must develop the airways across our own country . . . for purposes of defense.[10]

Always in civil aviation there was a political security element and vestiges of that abide even today: but this is to trespass on the next section. Instead of doing that it is important to focus on the third reason for dramatic change in the fortunes of the

US civil aviation industry and that means looking at the entrepreneurs who made it all possible. Most important of whom for present purposes is Juan Trippe of Pan Am because by 1939 Pan Am had an effective monopoly on US overseas routes.[11]

The story of Trippe and Pan Am is important because it tells us a great deal about the technical and economic challenges facing civil aviation in the inter-war period. Without airmail subsidies Pan Am and most other US and foreign airlines could not have flourished. But, while that was a necessary prerequisite for financial sustainability, it was not sufficient to guarantee success. Airlines had to have equipment fit for purpose for their huge ambition to cross the oceans and there had to be adequate supporting navigational capabilities (the political requirements are left to the next section). It is not possible here to provide a full account of the changes that were necessary for international aviation to develop in the way that it did in the inter-war period, but a series of snapshots of specific developments should convey a clear enough impression of what was needed and what kinds of things had to be done.

Juan Trippe gradually developed Pan Am into the US chosen instrument for overseas routes. That status was not official, but *de facto* it applied, as the British Secretary of State for Air, Lord Swinton, observed in 1937:

> Pan American Airways were the chosen instrument of the United States Government who, in effect, give them complete political and financial backing, although, when it suits their purpose, the Government puts forward the Company as an entirely independent commercial organisation.[12]

Along the route to his success, Trippe had two huge achievements to his credit.

Firstly, he and his company successfully adapted and built on navigational innovations championed by the US Army Air Service/Corps and US Navy. The Army Air Service/Corps pioneered long-distance flights, with lieutenants O.G. Kelly and J.A. Macready successfully traversing the continental USA non-stop in 1923 in a Fokker T-2. The key to success in long-distance flights was the earth inductor compass, patented in 1912 and refined successively in the early 1920s by the National Bureau of Standards and the Pioneer Instrument Company of New York. Using it in 1924 the Army Air Corps circumnavigated the world and other human and technological achievements soon followed. Notably Lindbergh in 1927 used an earth induction compass to navigate to Paris. It was within this context that Trippe and his colleagues recognized the importance of developing secure navigational aids – among other things to locate island refueling ports of call, most notably Wake Island in the vast reaches of the Pacific. In the 1930s, building upon past American technological advances, Pan Am helped to develop better technologies of navigation such as the gyroscopic heading indicator.

Secondly, Trippe had clear and wonderful vision for fit-for-purpose equipment, which he acquired by working closely with American aircraft manufacturers Sikorsky, Glenn Martin and later Boeing. When Trippe wrote to the six leading US manufacturers in 1931 asking them to produce an aircraft with a range of 2,500 miles and capable of carrying 300 pounds of mail, four of them replied that it was a pipe dream: two, however, did not – Glenn Martin and Sikorsky. Sikorsky delivered and the S42 met Trippe's specifications.

Effective long-range mail delivery was now a reality, but Sikorsky's triumph was eclipsed in October 1935 when Glenn Martin delivered its first M-130 to Pan Am. Christened the China Clipper, it had a range of 3,200 miles. It cruised at 163 miles an hour and could carry 43 passengers or 18 in sleeper configuration. As a result of navigational innovations and securing refueling stops through political maneuvering, the China Clipper was able to service the Philippines via Honolulu, Midway Island, Wake Island and Guam. It was a distance of nearly 7,000 miles. That same year Imperial Airways started a regular service from London to Brisbane, a distance of 12,722 miles, but it took 10 days in short hops with equipment inferior to the Martin-130 and without the navigational challenge of traversing the Pacific. The truth was that together the US, Trippe and Glenn Martin had stolen the lead in long-range passenger travel. The flagship of Imperial Airways, the Short C class Flying Boat, might have been the ultimate in luxury air travel, but was designed to hop along Britain's imperial routes where no leg was much longer than 500 miles. Soon that looked woefully inadequate once the prospect of flying across the Atlantic became an imminent possibility.[13] Again it was American technology and Trippe's entrepreneurship that consummated that hope. This time it was a Boeing aircraft, the 314, christened variations of Clipper, which first flew via the Azores to Marseilles on 9 May 1939, followed soon after with services via the northern Newfoundland route into Southampton.[14]

By 1939, in the US at least, the technological breakthrough in equipment necessary for long-distance passenger services had been made. The acceleration of technological advancement driven by war would build on that with hugely enhanced capability available by 1945. Paralleling these developments were advances in navigational aids.

The development of navigational aids was haphazard and sporadic and very primitive at times. In 1921 when the RAF ran a mail service between Cairo and Baghdad, a plough was used to mark out a navigational direction aid through part of the 400 miles of featureless desert over which the planes flew. Navigational aids developed in different ways in different countries with varying levels of government support. Within the United States, after the Morrow Board's report, large sums – over $60 million – were invested in infrastructure and navigation. US cities began to compete with each other for air traffic and the result was a huge injection of investment into municipal airports, paid for by local tax dollars.[15] In fact little funding actually came from the federal government (apart from airmail subsidies), but the US Weather Bureau did provide weather forecasts. For international routes the story was very different. Here it was largely left to Pan Am, albeit building on pioneering work by the US Army Air Corps and the cutting-edge navigational aids that it had used. Hugo C. Leuteritz, who worked closely with Trippe, was the brain behind some of the most innovative navigational developments, including Morse code for communication, as equipment for voice communications was too cumbersome for early aircraft, and direction finders that triangulated positions from ocean-going ships. In the end Pan Am did the logical thing and established a subsidiary company to manufacture radio and navigational equipment. Meanwhile in Latin America, where it had a huge route network, Pan Am again decided to do it itself. 'A chain of 93 radio and weather stations, some placed in remote mountain passes, was built to support Pan America's Latin American system, the largest private radio network in the world.'[16]

By the late 1930s Pan Am dominated US overseas routes. Much of this was because of its own industry, innovation and visionary leadership, but it was also riding on the back of government support in particular via the airmail system; its relationship with government went much further than just that. Over the years Trippe built up one of the most effective lobbying systems in the US Congress to champion the interests of Pan Am. US Senator Owen Brewster was commonly referred to as the Senator from Pan Am. The company also worked closely, though not always easily, with the State Department to obtain traffic rights; although for example in the case of Pan Am's exclusive US rights in the Azores the company negotiated directly with the Portuguese.[17] Pan Am also collaborated with the US Navy to establish refueling and servicing stops for its long-haul flights; most notably this applied to the developments on Wake Island in the Pacific. And finally, as war approached and then in the period between its outbreak and Pearl Harbor, Pan Am was engaged by the US government to help develop strategic routes in the event war should come to the US. No wonder Pan Am was seen as the chosen instrument of the US for its overseas airline routes. But this is leading into the realms of politics and governance, on which the full focus now needs to fall, first by examining some of the broad and generic factors involved and then by looking at the fraught politics of Anglo-American maneuvering to open transatlantic routes.

Responding to the challenges of politics and governances

Bilateralism was at the heart of international aviation in the inter-war period, but the Paris Convention did address and deal effectively with certain technical issues, such as aircraft registration and airworthiness. And these standards were applied in Europe, but not in the Americas. That was not an issue while there was no, or at least very little, transatlantic activity, but once the prospect of regular commercial crossings loomed then it was. In those circumstances states had to resort to bilateral agreements such as the one struck between the US and the UK in 1934 when they extended reciprocal recognition to each other's standards of flying competence and airworthiness.[18] The Paris Convention also established a permanent body, the ICAN, the main responsibility of which was to collect and disseminate information and make recommendations for further development of the Convention. The kind of information ICAN supplied in its weekly *Bulletin of Information* neatly demonstrates how rudimentary the whole industry was in the inter-war period. Airlines were requested to note in one issue that:

> sheep are grazing on the landing field at Le Bourget and planes should be careful to avoid them; that the Cherbourg-Querqueville Aerodrome will

be occupied by military formations on certain dates and private planes are barred; that plowing and leveling operations are in progress on the Croydon Aerodrome [the main London airport at the time] and pilots should avoid taxying beyond the boundary lights.[19]

So, here were the beginnings of the international dissemination of information, of data collection, uniformity on the technical side and also of an international bureaucracy concerned specifically with international civil aviation. Unfortunately, universal reach remained elusive and the ICAN had only very limited impact.

In the Americas there was no counterpart to the Paris Convention until the Havana Convention on Commercial Aviation of 1928.[20] Unlike the Paris Convention it did not create a permanent body nor were there any technical annexes. There was talk of a commercial regime, but it was never consummated. The main points to emphasize are that there now existed two different conventions purporting to provide some governance of technical and safety standards for the airline industry, which were not fully compatible, and that whereas the ICAN at least opened up the principle of more robust ongoing regulation via a permanent body, the Havana Convention did not. The system, if one could distinguish it so, was already fragmented even in the supposedly non-political areas of technical and safety standards. This was not a good augury.

In addition to the Paris and Havana Conventions, there were two other sources of governance and regulatory control in the inter-war period: the IATA and the Warsaw Convention. The work of the latter can be summarized in the words of one scholar as follows:

> In 1929, the Convention for the Unification of Certain Rules regarding International Air Transport was signed in Warsaw. The purpose of the Convention was to regulate in a uniform manner the conditions of international carriage by air including inter alia, documents of carriage and *the liability of carriers*. The above was the major international legislation on international aviation before the Chicago Convention of 1944 [emphasis added].[21]

The Warsaw Convention, and especially its provisions on liability, have been long lasting, though at times contentious, and are major legacies of the inter-war period, which proved largely barren otherwise. The Convention has gone through various amendments and additions – the Hague Protocol of 1955, the Guadalajara Convention of 1961, the Montreal Agreement of 1966 between IATA airlines and the US Civil Aeronautics Board (CAB) for flights into and out of the USA, the Guatemala Protocol of 1971 and protocols at Montreal in 1975. Finally, the latter was supplemented by the 1999 Montreal Convention, more of which in Chapter 4.

Airline representatives from six European countries founded the IATA at The Hague in August 1919. It was a mutual-help association open to all airlines subject to approval by existing members. Its *de facto* role became that of facilitating the commercial organization of European air services by coordinating schedules, timetables and conditions of carriage, and by standardizing documentation. Even as late as 1939 the membership was still overwhelmingly European, though Pan Am had joined in 1938 and there was a sprinkling of airlines from South America, Africa and Asia. Its contributions were significant in Europe, but marginal elsewhere. Its operations were suspended on the outbreak of war, but the IATA office continued in existence in The Hague until the first IATA was superseded by the second IATA, the International Air Transport Association, in 1945, which was based in Montreal.

Apart from bilateral agreements, this was the sum total of provision for international civil aviation in the inter-war period. To say that it was rudimentary is something of an understatement. But if lack of technical provisions is seen as a stumbling block for the development of inter-war aviation then the political problems that afflicted the industry must be described as a veritable mountain to climb. The main generic problems were and still are the interconnection between civilian and military air power and the problem of sovereignty. In the inter-war period this resulted in predatory bilateralism.

Some countries were simply obstructive, as Imperial Airways found to its cost. Britain aimed to develop two great imperial routes: one running to and through Africa to Cape Town and the other out to Asia and eventually on to Australia, New Zealand, Canada and the Atlantic *en route* back to Britain, thus creating an imperial round-the-world service. For the leg between Australia and Canada to be possible however Imperial Airways needed landing rights in Hawaii, something the US government refused to concede. Difficulties with transit and stop were commonplace; for example there were endless problems for Imperial Airways with Italy. Initially the eastern route to Asia ran through Italy with a mixture of train and air services, but within months difficulties with the Italian government pushed Imperial Airways into a large detour. Starting in November 1929 Imperial flew via Cologne, Vienna, Budapest and Belgrade to Athens, avoiding Italy altogether. Between May and October 1931 flights over Italy were reinstated only to be halted again because of recurring difficulties with the Italian government, which forced Imperial Airways this time to resort to train services through Italy. Such difficulties were by no means confined to Italy or Imperial Airways and they could only be resolved, or not as the case might be, by bilateral negotiations often drawing in matters extraneous to civil aviation. This was a jungle where only the powerful could survive: thriving was a lucky bonus.

This system of highly politicized bargaining for commercial rights was replicated in the western hemisphere, though with one airline clearly dominant: Pan Am, generally aided and abetted by the US government. But Trippe also knew how to pull pressure levers all on his own, as he amply demonstrated once Pan Am's route to Manila was established. He then wanted to extend it by entering the British colony of Hong Kong and fly on into China by connecting with his subsidiary China National Airways Corporation.[22] However, at first the British refused access to Hong Kong unless the US would reciprocate by granting them entry into Hawaii to provide a staging post for their own attempts to bridge the Pacific. Washington baulked at this on the pretext that they could not grant Britain such a right and refuse it to others, most notably the Japanese.[23] What they really objected to was the possibility of losing their dominant position in civil aviation in the Pacific and to Britain developing a round-the-world route. For a time, Trippe was thus unable to make headway, but he soon developed a strategy that persuaded Britain to open Hong Kong unilaterally. In 1937 Trippe negotiated landing rights in Macau with the Portuguese and then raised the specter of outmaneuvering the British in Hong Kong by developing Macau as a great civil aviation commercial hub for entry into China. 'As a result', Trippe later explained, 'we were invited to Hong Kong . . . . From that day we stayed there.'[24] Such politicking epitomized what Realists see as the anarchy of power moves in the international realm and that picture conjures up not only this kind of cutthroat practice in commerce, but also aviation's connection with security matters. Those were articulated most clearly at the Disarmament Conference in Geneva between 1932 and 1934.

Sir Hugh Montague 'Boom' Trenchard, commander of the British Royal Flying Corps (RFC) in France during World War One and father of the RAF, observed in 1916:

> Owing to the unlimited space in the Air, the difficulty one machine has in seeing another, the accident of wind and cloud, it is impossible for aero-planes, however skillful and vigilant their pilots, however numerous their formations, to prevent hostile aircraft from crossing the line if they have the initiative and determination to do so.[25]

It is never easy to trace the origin and interaction of ideas that result in full-blown strategic doctrines, but there is little doubt that the ideas of Trenchard and the Italian Giulio Douhet seeped through much of the strategic thinking in the inter-war years. Douhet, who is generally recognized as the first major theorist of air power, with his 1921 book *The Command of the Air*, emphasized the importance of bombing and its ability to inflict terror on the enemy population and undermine its morale.[26] These ideas had taken hold by the time of the Disarmament Conference and British Prime Minister Stanley Baldwin, echoing the same sentiments uttered by Trenchard, now spoke for many when he opined: 'The bomber will always get through.'[27] What was not spoken of quite so much in public was the growing fear, especially in France and Britain, that disarmament of military air power would be ineffective unless civil aircraft were regulated and controlled as well. In fact, the British government came to believe that effective control of civil aviation was a *sine qua non* of effective disarmament in the air.

The Geneva Conference was a sad and dispiriting affair. It took place against the backdrop of Japan's military aggression in Manchuria and its withdrawal from the League in 1933 and the coming to power of Hitler in Germany that same year. It is doubtful that either country under any circumstance would have agreed to comprehensive disarmament. Those countries, which in principle might have, were unable to build in enough reassurance that disarmament would work for it to be acceptable. There were all kinds of problems revolving around the security dilemma. For the British the Royal Navy was a defensive weapon; that was not how others saw it. The French wanted disarmament, but only if there were adequate guarantees and enforcement provisions – both of which ultimately depended on agreement by and active collaboration from the US, neither of which was forthcoming. And Germany bridled at the fact that it had been disarmed in accordance with Versailles, but other countries and most importantly France had not. Progress was thus highly unlikely from the outset; however, the discussions prompted by Geneva helped to develop thoughts about civil aviation and its possible future.

Gradually as the debates, proposals and counterproposals went on, it became clear that air power was one of the most intractable problems the conference confronted. The British felt vulnerable, maybe not so much as the French, but they worried about the relative decline of their military power. With regard to air power they ranked fifth in the world after being pre-eminent at the end of the war. France held a 2:1 superiority over Britain in the air. This led some of the more idealistic in the British government to advocate comprehensive air disarmament. Furthermore, the notion of comprehensive disarmament embraced the necessity of regulating civil aviation as well as banning aerial warfare.[28] In 1932 a paper entitled 'Draft Convention for the Abolition of Military Aircraft and the Internationalisation of Civil Aviation' was circulated among government ministers.[29] For those who saw civil aviation as a potential means to military power there were two options: either ban all states from operating international services and instead create an international airline that would service the world; or create a powerful international regulatory body, which would control national airlines. These ideas gained traction in France and in some quarters in the UK and resonated with the original debate about aviation instigated by the international jurists in the nineteenth century.

The debates in Geneva about aviation continued intermittently, but there were two persistent problems. The first was the position of the US. As a non-member of the League of Nations, it was never fully engaged at Geneva because the League would oversee any agreement that issued from the conference and the US was still wary of entanglement and being drawn willy-nilly into European conflicts via League actions. It had refused to ratify the Versailles Treaty on those grounds (though there were other reasons as well). The senior US representative at Geneva in June 1932 indicated that the US would not object to a European scheme of air disarmament, but it was clear it would not be party to such an agreement and moreover the US opposed the idea of regulating civil aviation as part of overall disarmament. This became even clearer in the Hoover Plan, which proposed the abolition of military planes but offered no comment on civilian when they had now become of central concern to many in Europe.[30] By the summer of 1933 it was clear delegates were chasing a chimera. A member of the British delegation reported back to London that the abolition of air forces now seemed a 'distant idea' and:

> Nor is there any possibility of agreement on the allied question of internationalization of civil aviation and international air police force, both of which under repeated examination in the United Kingdom have so far been shown to be impractical.[31]

Geneva ended in abject failure, but it had raised important issues, demonstrating just how political international civil aviation had become. If further evidence were needed of just how politically complicated things had become, it was provided by the US and the UK, as they sought to establish transatlantic civil air services.

Transatlantic crossings and politically competitive bilateralism

Trying to negotiate transatlantic services between the US and Britain encapsulated many of the problems of inter-war bilateralism and parts of the hand each player held also resonated into the 1940s, namely American strength in terms of equipment and aggressive commercial airlines and Britain's strategic strength in controlling vast swathes of the globe and hence potential landing grounds for refueling on long-haul routes. Even between two increasingly friendly countries the discussions in the 1930s were confusing and complex. That was so because of a myriad of factors: sensitive political and security considerations; a commercial milieu in which profitable returns were expected to vary for each side; and also there was the added complication that Trippe and Britain's Imperial Airways under its Chairman Sir Eric Geddes and General Manager C.E. Woods Humphrey worked closely and often secretly together, at least in certain areas, developing policies and negotiating independently of their governments. Woods Humphrey was the driving force for Imperial Airways and between him and Trippe there developed an understanding that together their two airlines should dominate the Atlantic on the basis of what they referred to as a 'square deal', but these secret agreements did not always remain secret and came to be frowned on by governments, which eventually insisted on more say and more involvement.

A key factor that drew the British government more directly into Imperial Airways' affairs was Trippe's attempt to negotiate independently with the Dominion of Newfoundland for landing rights for the northern transatlantic route. He kept in close touch with Imperial Airways, but even so the talks with Newfoundland aroused concerns in Ottawa. Canada was fearful of being excluded from what was expected to be a very lucrative transatlantic operation if it became superfluous for route operations because of direct flights from the US to Newfoundland and on to Britain via Ireland. Ottawa alerted London to its fears, but Trippe's negotiations were brought to an end when Newfoundland fell into economic disarray and reverted back from Dominion to British Crown Colony status in December 1933. Thereafter the British government, in the shape of Sir Francis Shelmerdine, the Director General of Civil Aviation, and Sir Donald Banks, Director General of the Post Office, insisted on more direct government intervention and closer liaison with Woods Humphrey. This was unpalatable to Trippe because he thought that final agreement on a transatlantic route would now likely be subject to more government involvement and harsher conditions for approval.[32]

Not only might the British government prove problematic, but the interests and objectives of Pan Am and the US government were also far from being in entire accord. Unlike the US government, Pan Am as well as Imperial Airways and the British government wanted to exclude competition by restricting operations between Britain and the USA to Pan Am and Imperial Airways. The British would also exclude airlines of other European countries from servicing the Atlantic by denying them landing rights on both the northern and southern routes in Newfoundland and Bermuda respectively. Not only was this generally anticompetitive, but it was also exclusive of any other US airline, something that troubled officials in Washington, especially in the Post Office, which was required by law to have competitive bidding for the award of airmail contracts. The idea of any pooling arrangement or 'square deal' that apportioned airmail revenue would thus be unlawful in America so far as the US Post Office was concerned. Unfortunately without a 'square deal' agreement involving commercial collusion, Imperial Airways would not receive what it considered an adequate share of transatlantic airmail revenue. It would only harvest a fraction of the revenue taken by Pan Am because of the larger proportion of mail originating in the USA.[33] Understandably this type of possible commercial collusion was not palatable to most Americans or the US Post Office.

Planning for transatlantic air routes intensified when British officials arrived in Washington for discussions in December 1935. Led by Sir Donald Banks and including Shelmerdine, Woods Humphrey and representatives of Canada and Ireland, they engaged in talks with members of the US Interdepartmental Committee on Civil International Aviation, Chaired by Undersecretary of State R. Walton Moore and representatives of Pan Am. The understanding which eventually emerged looked to provide a 15-year permit to Imperial Airways and Pan Am for each to operate twice-weekly transatlantic services running from the USA to the UK via Canada, Newfoundland and Ireland on a northern route and/or from the USA via Bermuda and other country stops to the UK on a southern route. The other stops essentially meant refueling in the Azores and going on to landfall somewhere in southern Europe, but neither Pan Am nor Imperial Airways held rights in the Azores in 1935. In principle there was supposedly no exclusivity and also the understandings were based 'upon the principle of full reciprocity between the countries interested. They do not operate to exclude similar arrangements between the United States and other countries.'[34] It was hoped that experimental flights could take place in 1936 with the full service being inaugurated in 1937. This timetable turned out to be unduly optimistic.

In fact it soon emerged that the understandings reached in Washington had not resolved everything, including the division of spoils from airmail. Also, unknown to the US authorities, Trippe had already reached an understanding with Woods Humphrey. They had met in New York the week before the talks in Washington, and Trippe identified the difficulties that the US government would likely cause for their existing plans mutually to dominate transatlantic routes:

> In the first place, political considerations (particularly the importance of the large Italian and German votes of the forthcoming Presidential election) would make it quite impossible for the Government of the United States of America to contemplate the conclusion of a formal agreement with any

foreign Government on an exclusive basis. Moreover it seemed certain that the United States Postal authorities . . . would be debarred legally from entering into any agreement with regard to the mutual exchange of air mails in advance of the establishment of a service. . . . In these circumstances, Mr. Trippe and . . . [Woods Humphrey] were agreed that the best . . . approach would be to continue negotiations between the two Companies with a view to producing a basis of common agreement.[35]

A month later on 25 January 1936, Woods Humphrey in London and Trippe in New York signed, on a company-to-company basis, an agreement for each to fly two round trips a week on the northern route via Newfoundland. They were to enjoy exclusive rights, neither could start till the other did, and everything was to be on the basis of a square deal that would among other things take care of Britain's disadvantage concerning revenue from airmail carriage.[36] US commitments to non-exclusivity seemed to have been negated and US law transgressed.

Meanwhile on 22 February the British Air Ministry issued Pan Am with a permit to fly in and out of the UK, Newfoundland and Bermuda. On 5 March a similar permit was issued to Pan Am by the Canadian authorities and on 13 April Ireland followed suit. The permits were handed to Trippe on 20 April in the Commerce Department in Washington, DC. Simultaneously Trippe had been negotiating with the Portuguese government on a company-to-government basis and had managed to extract from it permits to use the Azores for 25 years with a clause excluding any other American airline for 15 years. The British negotiated similar rights, but Pan Am clearly looked triumphant with the way now open on the northern and southern transatlantic routes to Europe.

Basking in his strong position, Trippe in March 1938 explained to Woods Humphrey that the square deal that looked to pooling airmail revenue and which stipulated that neither side would start the transatlantic service until the other was ready was compromising him politically in Washington. The result was that Woods Humphrey agreed to amend their agreement and delete both the pooling arrangements and the simultaneous start.[37] This did not mean, however, that one side could necessarily start without the other. With the passage of the US Civil Aeronautics Act in June 1938, Imperial Airways would have to be approved by the new regulator created by the act, the CAB and by the President before operations could begin. And, for their part, the British with their control over Bermuda and Newfoundland would always have the last say on whether airlines flew the Atlantic or not. At least that was the case until early 1939.

In early 1939 after protracted talks with the French, the United States took the first step to outmaneuver the British in their control of Atlantic routes. They announced that France had been awarded landing rights in the USA for a six-month period and the draft agreements were exchanged in March.[38] That in itself was not sufficient to undermine Britain's ability to control the Atlantic routes, but when combined with the range of the new Boeing 314 it was. The Boeing 314 had a range of 3,500 miles, which was enough to allow it to bypass Bermuda and land at the Azores in one hop, refuel and fly on to Marseilles. In March 1939 after problems and delays Boeing finally started deliveries to Pan Am. This not only meant that Britain was outmaneuvered it also cast into gloom the picture of British equipment. The British had managed to fly the first transatlantic commercial flight to Canada when the Short-Mayo composite carried a small package of mail from Foynes to Montreal 21–22 July 1938. This was a rather strange pick-a-back plane: a large flying boat carried a smaller one aloft, which then took off in flight, but it had only tiny cargo capacity. Britain's other available planes, the Empire Flying Boats, could only traverse the Atlantic with in-flight refueling and the De Havilland land plane that was supposed to be an alternative, rather appropriately named Albatross, sadly broke up on landing in an early test flight.[39] The British could not compete effectively, but they knew when they had been outmaneuvered and with war now imminent they were not willing to antagonize the USA by delaying Pan Am's transatlantic operations any further. They announced this in the House of Commons on 1 February.[40] Just over a week later, Trippe, realizing that the transatlantic route was almost within his grasp, took one further step to appease a growing band of critics within the US who took exception to his monopolistic tendencies.

The US Civil Aeronautics Authority (the precursor of the CAB) was directed by the 1938 Civil Aeronautics Act to consider competition to be in the public interest to the extent necessary to assure the industry's sound development, which raised the issue of Pan Am's exclusive access deal to the Azores with the Portuguese government.[41] In early February Trippe thought it prudent to make the following statement:

> If the Civil Aeronautics Authority will confirm our understanding that it is now of the opinion that it would be in the interest of American aviation that Clause 3 [i.e. the 15-year exclusivity clause] of the agreement of this Company with the Portuguese Government be waived, our company will advise the Government promptly that it waives such Clause 3 in its entirety.[42]

The letter was given considerable publicity and concerns about Pan Am's agreement with Portugal were largely assuaged. On the evening of 18 May 1938 President Roosevelt signed off on the route certificates and on 20 May and 24 June, respectively, Pan Am inaugurated regular mail and passenger services on the southern and northern routes. All that Imperial Airways could manage was eight mail flights by in-flight refueled Empire Flying Boats in August and September, after which operations were suspended because of the outbreak of war.[43]

Conclusion

In many ways it is astonishing that civil aviation progressed as far as it did in the inter-war period. At the outbreak of World War Two transatlantic services had been inaugurated and the industry was poised on the cusp of great possibilities. Boeing produced the first all-metal structure airplane with cantilever wings and retractable undercarriage in 1933: it was the harbinger of the modern age of passenger aircraft. Boeing followed that up in 1938 with the first plane with a pressurized cabin, the Boeing 307 Stratoliner. In Germany Heinkel flew the first turbojet powered plane, the He 178, in August 1939. The world had been circumnavigated and the oceans crossed by solo fliers. Imperial Airways ran a passenger service from Britain to Brisbane and Pan Am serviced the Pacific and launched regular transatlantic services in 1938. Technology and navigational challenges no longer held long-haul passenger services in check. Both had seen huge advances in the 1930s and things were to accelerate even more rapidly with the onset of war. However, for the time being the war either put an end to or seriously inconvenienced normal passenger services across the globe.

Appropriate technology and navigational infrastructure were both essential prerequisites for international civil aviation's achievements in the inter-war period, but they were not sufficient: the world needed capable international airlines. That requirement was only met by government support, not only of the infrastructure, but also of the airlines themselves. Subsidies and chosen instruments for overseas operations were the hallmark of the development of international civil aviation and would remain so for decades with the exception of the US after 1945. Without government support the development of American airlines was stymied and they languished in the 1920s well behind their European counterparts. The story was similar in Britain. By 1922 the British airline industry had collapsed in the face of foreign and particularly French airline competition that was heavily subsidized. It was only after government money was pumped into the fledgling British airline industry that it again began to make progress. Similarly in the US, until the Kelly and subsequent acts of Congress provided funding and therefrom a source of financial stability, US airlines struggled. After the Kelly Act, they thrived and soon became world leaders. Government finance was essential in the 1920s and 1930s for the development of effective airlines. Financial sustainability in this period meant central and local government financial help of all kinds – direct and indirect subsidies – and money for infrastructure.

The result in the international sphere of aviation was the emergence of state-owned or sponsored airlines, which were heavily subsidized for prestige, status, commercial and security reasons and as a means to link imperial and colonial possessions together. The US case was somewhat different in that Pan Am was a private company not in receipt of direct subsidies, but *de facto* it differed little from airlines such as Imperial Airways: it did have widespread government support and was effectively the US chosen instrument for overseas routes. Government motives for supporting their own country's airline or airlines distorted the market through subsidies, predatory pricing and the extraction of preferential and discriminatory operating rights.

The relative failure of the Paris and Havana Conventions to create a uniform set of standards for safety, technical and international infrastructure and their abject failure to deal effectively with the commercial needs of the international airline system delivered it into the hands of individual nation states and whatever bilateral agreements they could reach. This is a slight exaggeration because some matters were dealt with more comprehensively and were not restricted to bilateralism.

The key example of that is the Warsaw Convention. So there were some multilateral provisions, modest attempts at standardization of technical and safety standards. There was also the creation of an embryonic international bureaucracy with vested interests in the industry, which could develop contrary to parochial national interests, but, generally speaking, bilateralism was rampant and the dominant feature of the system.

Under certain circumstances, as was the case after 1946, bilateralism can operate in a relatively orderly fashion: in the inter-war period that was not the case. Airlines and their patron governments had to struggle through negotiation after negotiation in attempts to secure rights of transit and technical stop, never mind securing commercial outlets. Further complicating this was the fact that on numerous occasions airlines conducted their own 'diplomatic' negotiations. In the 1930s the British government reined in Imperial Airways, but Pan Am continued unabated in its dealings with foreign governments, at least until political feeling in Washington turned against it decisively during the war and it was decided that negotiations should be in the hands solely of the State Department. While the potential for international passenger and mail services remained small, the world could get by with this dysfunctional system, but when greater opportunities beckoned, as they were starting to at the onset of war, then incentives grew for crafting a more commercially friendly regime.

Many were aware of the problems and dangers of predatory bilateralism in the 1930s, but it was difficult to see any solution. During the war, planners in the US and the UK, and elsewhere, searching for a blueprint for a better world, took up the challenge recognizing that, above all else, civil aviation suffered from politics. To build a more commercial system that would allow expansion and airlines to thrive without undue government hindrance would require solutions to many intractable problems. Those problems had been chewed over endlessly at the Geneva Disarmament Conference but to little avail, except to highlight the difficulty of achieving consensus on what to do. Idealists had tabled ideas for untying the Gordian knot that bound civil aviation to air sovereignty, most specifically through internationalization, and that idea seemed attractive, but finding a practical version acceptable to all proved elusive because of the growing conviction of how important civil aviation was to the development of military air power.

As war approached the importance of civil aviation and security was emphasized by a growing public and official conviction about the vulnerabilities of civilian populations to attack from the air. On 26 April 1937 German warplanes destroyed Guernica and provided horrifying, albeit exaggerated, evidence of the dangers of civilian obliteration from the air. That same year UK official estimates indicated probable deaths in the order of 600,000 and injuries to 1,200,000 in the first 60 days of a war. There was a consensus that indeed the bomber would always get through and that such rapid carnage would result in a quick collapse of the enemy's morale and will to fight. Such thinking led to strategic readiness by the RAF to engage in area bombing that inevitably resulted in high civilian enemy casualties. In retrospect however it is clear that the bomber did not in fact always get through and the strategic doctrines that came to prevail in the Second World

War raised many questions about the possibility of waging war according to traditional just war principles.[44] But this is in retrospect and so far as civil aviation was concerned at the time the real fears about air warfare placed civil aviation squarely within broad and intractable security concerns.

It was partly because of such security fears that wartime planners revisited internationalization as a way of dealing with civil aviation's potential to contribute to a nation's air power. They conceived of internationalization in various forms ranging from the creation of an internationally owned airline that would provide all international services to forms of international regulation of national airlines. Furthermore, internationalization was now seen not only as a measure linked with disarmament and security and a way of cutting the Gordian knot that bound states to air sovereignty, but also by many as a possible foil for likely US domination of international civil aviation. But, in the meantime, bilateralism remained the dominating characteristic of international civil aviation, though all turned to turmoil with the onset of war in Europe and its ever expanding reach to become truly worldwide.

Notes

1 John Maynard Keynes, *The Economic Consequences of the Peace*, London: Macmillan, 1920, pp. 26 and 29.
2 J.W.S. Branker, *IATA and What It Does*, Leyden: Sitjhoff, 1977, p. 7.
3 I am indebted in this section, and elsewhere, to my friend Peter Hugill, who gently corrected some of my misapprehensions about technological and infrastructure developments.
4 Carl Solberg, *Conquest of the Skies: A History of Commercial Aviation in America*, Boston: Little Brown and Co., 1979, p. 63.
5 *Ibid.*, 74; *Franklin D. Roosevelt Library*, Hyde Park, New York (hereafter FDRL) FDR Official File (OF)249, box 1, Folder: Aeronautics March–April 1934, Air Transport Facts Published by Aeronautical Chamber of Commerce of America.
6 *FDRL*, FDR OF 2955, box 2, CAB 1938–1942, folder: CAB 1938, Clinton Hester radio speech, 18 July 1938.
7 Peter J. Hugill, *World Trade Since 1431*, Baltimore and London: John Hopkins University Press, 1993, p. 266, citing British National Archives (hereafter BNA) AVIA2/1911.
8 British Government Command Paper 1739, *First Report on the Imperial Air Mail Service*, 1922 and J.A. Cross, *Sir Samuel Hoare: A Political Biography*, London: Jonathan Cape, 1977.
9 Robert Bluffield, *Imperial Airways: The Birth of the British Airline Industry 1914–1940*, Hersham: Ian Allan, 2009.
10 R.L. Wilbur and H.M. Hyde, *The Hoover Policies*, New York: Scribner's, 1937, pp. 215–18.
11 There are numerous works dealing with Juan Trippe and Pan Am, the best of which are: Marylin Bender and Selig Altschul, *The Chosen Instrument: Pan Am, Juan Trippe, the Rise and Fall of an American Entrepreneur*, New York: Simon and Schuster, 1982; and Robert Daley, *An American Saga: Juan Trippe and His Pan Am Empire*, New York: Random House, 1980. I have drawn liberally on these works for this study.
12 *Canadian National Archives*, Ottawa, (hereafter *CNA*) Papers of W.L. Mackenzie King, MG26 J4, reel C4266, Imperial Conference Records C126051–C126203, Committee on Civil Air Communications, Sub-Committee on the Trans-Tasman and Trans-Pacific Services, 1st meeting 3 June 1937.

13 Germany also had some restricting technical problems. The Dornier Do X was the largest plane in the world in 1929 when the prototype was produced and the largest flying boat during the inter-war period. It flew the Atlantic from Germany to New York between November 1930 and August 1931. Unfortunately its twelve engines were too energy hungry and the weight of fuel required only allowed it a short range. Commercially it was unviable. The same could be said of Short's ingenious answer to the C class flying boat's short range – the Short-Maia composite involving a piggy-back operation whereby a Short flying boat carried the Maia aloft, carried it to its range capacity and then the Maia was launched to continue on. By this means a small amount of mail was carried across the Atlantic.

14 See Daley, *An American Saga*. One of the ways that airline infrastructure costs were kept low for international travel in the 1930s was by the use of flying boats, which did not require expensive landing grounds.

15 See Janet Rose Daley Bednarek, *America's Airports: Airfield Developments, 1918–1947*, College Station: Texas A&M University Press, 2001.

16 Bender and Altschul, *The Chosen Instrument*, p. 163.

17 Trippe decided it prudent to relinquish his exclusive rights prior to inaugurating Pan Am's transatlantic service because of political pressures.

18 *Foreign Relations of the United States (FRUS)*, 1929, vol. 1, Washington DC, US Government Printing Office, p. 539 editorial comment.

19 Quoted from Colgrove, *International Control of Aviation*, p. 31.

20 In 1926, Spain, having withdrawn from the League of Nations, made a bid for influence in Latin America by calling an Ibero-American Air Navigation Convention, but it was a failure.

21 Richard Y. Chuang, *The International Air Transport Association*, Leiden: Sijthoff, 1972, p. 17.

22 A. Sampson, *Empires of the Sky: The Politics, Contests and Cartels of World Airlines*, London: Hodder and Staughton, 1984, p. 59.

23 Hawaii was a crucial landing base for the British. They tried to bargain landing rights in Fiji for Pan American's route to Australia in return for rights into Hawaii, but again the Americans refused and Pan American developed a staging post at Pago Pago in the American Samoan Islands: see Sampson, *Empires of the Sky*, p. 59.

24 *Smithsonian National Aeronautical and Space Museum Archives*, Washington DC, *Trippe Papers*, box 1, Trippe address to Foreign Service Association, 24 February 1966; Daley, *American Saga*, p. 182.

25 RFC HQ memorandum 22 September 1916, quoted from M.J. Armitage and R.A. Mason, *Air Power in the Nuclear Age, 1954–84: Theory and Practice*, Basingstoke: Macmillan 1985, p. 4.

26 Giulio Douhet, *The Command of the Air*, New York: Arno Press, 1942.

27 Stanley Baldwin, in the House of Commons as reported by *The Times*, 11 November 1932.

28 The Hague Draft Rules for Aerial Warfare 1923 had attempted to impose constraints on air warfare, but without success. At Geneva the ambition was greater, but suffered a similar fate.

29 *BNA* CAB 26/39, CP(32)164, 26 May 1932.

30 E.L. Woodward and R. Butler (editors), *Documents on British Foreign Policy 2nd Series vol. 4*, London: HMSO, 1950, pp. 606–68.

31 Woodward and Butler, *British Foreign Policy*, vol. 4, pp. 279–80, Babbington to Simon, 29 May 1933.

32 *Trippe Papers*, box 20, 'History of Transatlantic Air Service', 17–18; *BNA* FO 371/19635, ICIAC minutes 19 June 1935; *FRUS*, 1935, volume 1, 510–19, Hull to Ambassador Bingham, 24 April 1935 and minutes of meeting, Moore, Trippe et al., 6 May 1935.

33 *BNA*, CAB 24/257, CP(35)222, joint memorandum by Chancellor of the Exchequer Chamberlain and Secretary of State for Air Cunliffe-Lister (later Lord Swinton), 2 December 1935, which includes a summary of a report on 'Proposed Commonwealth Agreement for an Atlantic Air Service.'

34 *Ibid.*, 12 December meeting with British, Irish and Canadian delegations; press release by Moore, 12 December 1935; *USNA* 811.79640/120, statement by Moore, 12 December 1935.

35 *BNA*, CAB 24/259, CP(36)14, 'The Report of the UK Air Mission to North America November to December 1935', Donald Banks and F.C. Schelmerdine to Sir Warren Fisher, Chairman of Interdepartmental Committee on International Air Communications, 30 December, 1935.

36 Alan P. Dobson, *Peaceful Air Warfare: The United States, Britain, and the Politics of International Aviation*, Oxford: Clarendon Press, 1991, p. 119; Daley, *American Saga*, 208–9.

37 *Ibid.*, 229.

38 *Moore Papers FDRL*, box 2, folder: Civil Aeronautical Authority 1938 and 1939, *passim*. It should be noted that by 1938 it was the Germans who were best equipped and prepared to mount transatlantic operations between the USA and Europe, but the US government was not prepared to move forward with them.

39 *USNA*, 841.796/415 and /421, US Consul Southampton to State Department, 5 October 1938, and Johnson to Hull, 24 January 1939, enclosing clippings from *Daily Mail*, 21 January 1939.

40 *Hansard*, 1 February 1939, volume 343, column 187, Balfour.

41 *Moore Papers*, box 2, folder: Aviation, Civil Aeronautics Authority 1938 and 1939, undated draft for Moore to Pan American.

42 *FDRL* FDR PSF, box 115, folder: American Export Lines, Trippe to CAA 9 February 1939.

43 Daley, *American Saga*, pp. 228–9.

44 See Roger Ruston, *A Say in the End of the World: Morals and British Nuclear Policy 1941–1987*, Oxford: Oxford University Press, 1990, pp. 52–5.

3 Wartime planning and the Chicago Conference 1939–1944

Our two earliest studies of post-war civil aviation have recommended complete internationalisation. If by this is meant a kind of Volapuk Esperanto cosmopolitan organisation managed and staffed by committees of all peoples great and small with pilots of every country from Peru to China (especially China), flying every kind of machine in every direction, many people will feel that this is at present an unattainable ideal.[1]

Prime Minister Winston Churchill, June 1943

Introduction: the focus and the challenge

One of the most extraordinary things about the Second World War was the time, energy and resources devoted by the Allies to post-war planning and among the list of major topics covered was international civil aviation. It posed a huge challenge: how to create a commercial international regime that would allow airlines of the world to flourish whilst being compatible with different and conflicting national interests. As planning developed the debate centered on what are known as the Five Freedoms of the air: they provided for: (i) innocent passage or over-flight; (ii) technical stop for repairs or refueling; (iii) the right to pick up passengers from an airline's country of origin and disembark them in territory of the other contracting party; (iv) the right to pick up passengers in the other contracting country and disembark them in the airline's country of origin; and (v) the right to pick up passengers from the other contracting party and carry them forward to a third-party destination.[2] What the planners started in the Second World War led on to the kind of ambitions that now circulate round the industry, at least in some very influential quarters, and is known as globalization.

Prima facie aviation would seem a pre-eminent candidate for the early realization of a globalized market, but, as noted in the previous chapter, politics intruded to create an environment fragmented by sovereign airspace and national regulations, the very antithesis of globalization. A truly globalized airline industry would be a marketplace that was not fragmented by state boundaries and national regulations, where airlines made decisions on the provision and price of services primarily according to market conditions, and where common rules on competition, ownership, control and safety regulations would apply. All players would be playing the same game according to the same rules (i.e. on a level playing field). Vision did not stretch to this during the Second World War, but one could argue that the goal of globalization naturally emerged from what went on then and developed traction and it is important to bear this trajectory in mind when considering what follows in this and the following two chapters.

Commercial possibilities beckoned in a manner not possible in the inter-war period. They were now seen to be of colossal importance as a result of advances in technology and the wartime experience accumulated by civil airlines recruited for military purposes. Adolf A. Berle, the head of the US delegation at the Chicago International Civil Aviation Conference in 1944, spoke for many when he said: 'I feel that aviation will have a greater influence on American foreign interests and American foreign policy than any other non-political [*sic*] consideration.'[3] It was common to see the potential of civil aviation in the same order of importance as the role of the merchant marine in the nineteenth century. But, such commercial possibilities also connected in a more important way than ever with security, and that was nowhere better illustrated than in the US.

The war demonstrated the importance of civil aviation for manufacturing, pilot training and overseas logistics, all of which were crucial for the US war effort. President Roosevelt set a manufacturing target of 20,000 planes a year in September 1938, raised it to 50,000 in May 1940 and, at peak production in 1944, the figure actually achieved stood at around 100,000 planes a year. Such impressive numbers and the eventual quality of the planes would not have been possible without civil aviation's existing research, production and development capabilities.[4]

Similarly it was important to have trained pilots. The US CAB concluded in 1938 that the US should 'take immediate steps to strengthen its aviation resources unless it is to invite the ignominy and attendant grave national risk of becoming a second-rate power.'[5] Eventually with the robust backing of the president this led to the passage through Congress of the Civilian Pilot Training Scheme in June 1939. After American entry into the war it became the War Training Service and by 1944 over 400,000 pilots had been helped in their training under its auspices.[6]

Logistics were also crucial for the effective deployment of air power and again civil aviation played a vital role. After France's surrender in June 1940 the US planned a string of strategic air bases running from Canada down into Latin America.

Money provided 'for emergencies affecting the national security' by Public Laws 588, 611 and 703 of 1940 was funneled via the War Department and the Federal Loan Agency into Pan Am's coffers: 'officially the United States had no right to build bases in neutral nations anxious to stay out of any global conflict. But a privately owned airline could, and thus entered Pan Am.'[7] Not surprisingly a confidential memorandum for James Forrestal, Under Secretary of the Navy, declared the content of the plan 'political dynamite'.[8] The contract with Pan Am was signed secretly in November and over the next four years involved construction or improvement of over 50 air bases worldwide. And Pan Am was not the only US airline to provide essential logistical support for the military others included American Export Lines and Trans World Airlines (TWA).

All these security implications impacted on planning for post-war international civil aviation and especially so in the US: it was not possible to separate civil from military aviation.

In the inter-war period security concerns and the prevalence of a conservative view about air sovereignty hamstrung the development of international civil aviation. Rampant bilateralism made the granting of transit and technical stop subject to political interests and whimsy, creating an anarchically shifting and complex system where heavy subsidies were commonplace and predatory pricing a constant threat.

Discrimination, monopolization of routes and subsidized uneconomic operations often led to cutthroat competition, political friction and security fears. Wartime developments now threatened to exacerbate all this, creating a nationalistic security whirlpool that would suck under civil aviation unless some kind of international order could be created that would allay security concerns and allow the market to develop. In theory, there were several possible scenarios.

The first was the *status quo ante bellum*, but there was widespread recognition that this would be undesirable. It would seriously limit the growth of civil aviation, thereby reducing not only commercial gains, but also the industry's contribution to security. Always there was irony and paradox: as demonstrated at the Geneva Disarmament Conference, one country's security was another country's source of insecurity. Determining what was offensive and defensive depended on one's particular position and perspective and so it was with civil aviation. No country could now risk ignoring the development of civil aviation for fear of its development elsewhere and its potential contribution to military air power. The US with the immediate possibility of developing a huge and dominant world civil aviation industry at the war's end was loath to relinquish such an advantage for both commercial and defense prospects. The question was how to overcome the security dilemma with respect to international civil aviation? Britain the other key player in civil aviation also had inducements for reform. Its far-flung empire provided it with bases and routes that could be commercially exploited while also meeting the political need for empire communications. It also hoped to reap commercial rewards in Europe and felt a need to position itself closely to the US and to work towards finding a mutually acceptable solution to the existing dysfunctional system.[9] Both the US and Britain also recognized that if they did not develop civil aviation others would, to the commercial and security costs of both of them. Furthermore, there was a widespread view that the problem posed by international civil aviation was partly symptomatic of broader political dilemmas related to the creation of a lasting peace. Triumphs in the air made frontiers more permeable and brought a new poignancy to humanity's vulnerabilities and that explains why the future of civil aviation and collective security became linked. For some, civil aviation became a bellwether for what might be achieved more broadly for collective security. Elements of this had arisen at the Geneva

Disarmament Conference: the Second World War with area bombing practiced by all sides, culling huge numbers of civilian lives, simply gave them new emphasis. It was a combination of these reasons which created a compelling sense that the *status quo ante bellum* could not be allowed to endure.

A second option was to open the skies via the First and Second Freedoms, providing transit and technical stop to all airlines as of right, rather than something subject to political negotiation and extorted payments. In addition that would go hand in hand with international understandings on safety, weather forecasting, and navigational and technical standards of a kind that eventually became the remit of the United Nations' ICAO. This would not solve the problem of the anarchical and predatory commercial bilateralism of the inter-war period, but it would go a long way to delivering a uniform technical framework.

A third possibility was to combine the second option with the bilateral exchange of commercial rights, but with more orderly behavior than during the inter-war period, possibly by the creation of a model bilateral, which countries would be urged to follow by the system leader or leaders.[10]

A fourth possibility came in two guises, both of which would combine the second option with a multilateral commercial agreement. However for one variant that would be the full story, for the other there would be a further chapter involving a strong international body to regulate the commercial operations of airlines in the international sphere, including allocation of routes, passenger quotas, frequencies, capacity and the setting of fares.

A fifth possibility was the second option combined with the creation of an internationally owned airline that would have a monopoly on international services.

These five possibilities cover the ground from atavistic nationalism to progressive internationalism: from the conservative to a form of liberal-welfare collectivism. How they fared must now be the focus of attention.

Wartime planning before Chicago

The culmination of wartime aviation planning was the Chicago Conference. The Americans and the British, with some help from the Canadians, largely determined what went on there, but their positions had morphed through several stages in the lengthy run-up to the conference and there were stark disagreements both between the US and Britain and within US officialdom.[11]

By 1939 the US was already overwhelmingly dominant in civil aviation with its advanced equipment and possession of competitive airlines. In contrast Britain lagged behind because of, among other reasons, its need to concentrate on the development of military to the detriment of civil aircraft. Matters became more lop-sided in the war because of an agreed division of labor by which Britain left the production of transport aircraft to the US. Americans were thus well placed to expand their civil operations worldwide after the war, providing they could achieve agreement to open up the market. In contrast, Britain found itself weak and vulnerable and that inclined it to adopt defensive strategies. Britain would enter the post-war period bereft of competitive equipment and was tempted to ward off the threat of American domination of international civil aviation by tightly regulating the market. Notwithstanding its general weakness, it held a strong bargaining card in aviation, as it could threaten to exclude US airlines from vast swathes of the globe where Britain's say held sway if the US did not agree to some form of international regulation. In London in the summer of 1941 the first of a series of committees – successively Shelmerdine, Finlay and Barlow – began to explore post-war civil aviation possibilities.[12] All of them had internationalization and variations on that theme at their center.[13] As the Finlay Report put it:

> The choice before the world lies between Americanisation and internationalisation. If this is correct, it is difficult to doubt that it is under the latter system that British interests will best be served.[14]

This was not the Volapuk/Esperanto style of internationalization of which Churchill was so contemptuous; it was a prudent strategy to maximize British interests in the face of overwhelming US power. It is best understood as international regulation rather than internationalization. The British goal was to agree to a liberalization of the industry and make it more commercially viable with facilitated transit and stop rights and standardization of safety and technical matters: so far so good and in agreement with the Americans. But the British also insisted on making all that subject to rigid international controls, which would safeguard British commercial operations and ensure that they held a substantial market share. So, in order to resist the American threat, the pragmatists in London allied with idealistic elements in Whitehall and Westminster to promote various forms of internationalization as a way of protecting British interests and constraining American interests. These proposals ranged from the creation of an internationally and collectively owned company that would operate all international commercial aviation to various forms of regulation of the industry by an international authority, sometimes as part of a comprehensive system of collective world security. Leaders in London did not expect and most did not actually want the US to accept full-blown internationalization, but they were determined to press for as much movement down this route as would promote British interests.[15]

The American position was complex and buffeted by contending political demands. The idealism of Vice President Henry Wallace, for example, looked similar to the most idealist internationalist ideas that were circulating in London, but they came from very different motives: his idealism was not a mask for pragmatism. He argued for taking civil aviation out of the hands of private companies and internationalizing it. This was just about as radical as one could get and he promoted these ideas widely in newspaper and magazine articles.[16] Such idealism had traction in Australia, New Zealand, among an important faction in the Canadian Department of External Affairs led by Norman Robertson and Escott Reid and among idealists, often from the Labour Party, in Britain. It was, however, anathema to Trippe and his extreme nationalist allies such as Henry Luce who popularized 'the American Century' in 1941 as a way of encapsulating the contemporary and aspirational hegemonic destiny of the US. He was a powerful and influential man through his ownership of *Time, Life* and *Fortune* magazines. In the US elections of 1942 his wife Clare Booth Luce was elected to Congress for Fairfield County, Connecticut. Groomed by Trippe's lieutenant Sam Pryor she delivered her maiden speech on 9 February 1943. Entitled 'America's Destiny in the Air' her target was Wallace and internationalization and her promotion the American Century in the air:

> But much of what Mr. Wallace calls his global thinking is, no matter how you slice it, globaloney. Mr. Wallace's warp of sense and his woof of nonsense is very tricky cloth of which to cut the pattern of a post-war world.[17]

She spoke of the need for US airlines to fly everywhere in the post-war world and as American airlines, not as part of some crackpot scheme of internationalization. With a single word 'globaloney' she gained immediate celebrity status and sparked an international controversy about US intentions for post-war aviation. A few months later Trippe made it abundantly clear what he thought US policy should be. His position was predictable. He wanted nothing to do with multilaterally granting rights and automatic reciprocity and he feared that the benefits of a general exchange of transit and technical stop were more apparent than real.[18]

> We should keep ourselves free of any general commitments in favor of reciprocity, that we should seek landing rights without offering them, that we should handle requests for landing rights from countries that have granted them to us, on their merits, that in practice . . . we should successfully, and without jeopardizing our own position abroad, find plausible reasons to deny most requests and keep our concessions to a minimum.[19]

A better statement of the American imperial aviation position one would be hard pressed to find. This was the position of extremists in the US, but there were others, such as Lloyd Welch Pogue, the Chairman of the CAB, who did not go as far but who were nevertheless determined to safeguard US aviation strength internationally and thought that the US should therefore not 'give' too much away in negotiations.

The three key figures in the US administration who determined official policy were President Franklin Roosevelt, Adolf Berle, Assistant Secretary of State at the State Department, and Pogue. All three agreed that the pre-war monopoly of Pan Am had to be broken and other US airlines move out onto international routes. They felt something needed to be done to prevent subsidies except in exceptional cases and wanted to prevent predatory and other forms of unfair pricing. Roosevelt also liked Pogue's idea of allocating US airlines international sectors so that they would not compete directly with each other but only with foreign airlines and all three favored a multilateral agreement on transit and technical stop as a prerequisite for commercial operations. However, very serious differences lurked behind these agreements.

Berle was technically in charge of US international civil aviation, but Roosevelt set the general contours of policy and it was Pogue who chaired policy development committees, gathered data and interacted most with the industry and the Congress. Pogue in fact had a greater say in actual policy development than Berle, and ultimately more than the president. Unlike Berle, who was highly intelligent but abrasive, Pogue was intelligent and an effective political operator. He also held some radically different views to Roosevelt and it was how those played out that largely determined US policy and the outcome on commercial aviation matters in Chicago.

The Chicago Conference

Chicago was primarily the US government's attempt to rid the commercial international aviation system of the obstacles placed in its way by the kind of company maneuvering, political and security interests that had so complicated and restricted the industry in the inter-war period and which were at work in Imperial Airways' and Pan Am's attempts to launch transatlantic services in the 1930s.

The Chicago Conference was essentially about the relative wisdom of two options. The first involved strong international regulation of a multilateral aviation system for both technical-safety and economic sectors, championed primarily by Britain. The second option is more difficult to convey. The official US position promoted a regime that had only the lightest touch of international regulation with multilateral agreement for both the technical-safety sector and for the economic sector, which was to be based on agreement to automatically exchange the Five Freedoms. However, there was a variant on this favored by a faction led by Pogue, which was determined that the economic sector should be based on bilateralism and not multilateral agreement.

It should be pointed out that this picture of the US position exaggerates the absence of international regulation in one respect as it wanted some form of regulation for pricing. Certainly no senior US official ever favored free pricing and the role of IATA rate conferences, which eventually solved this problem, provided a form of international regulation. However, the US overall position was clearly and generally hostile to international regulation and once the Chicago Conference began it did not take long for the newspapers to pick up on some of the peculiarities of the US position. As one article put it: 'There is something of a logical boner at the bottom of the idea of calling a big international conference to agree to no international supervision.'[20]

There were two key issues which determined what happened at Chicago in the technical-safety and economic sectors. The first issue was differences between Britain and the US. As already explained, Britain was in a weaker position than the US, but no country can play the international civil aviation game alone. There always have to be willing partners and because of Britain's widespread geographical influence, the US would have to find some way forward to cooperate and the British knew that. The second issue involved differences within the US administration, which were reflected in its delegation at Chicago. The results of this configuration of power and ambition at Chicago were the International Transit Agreement and the Provisional ICAO (PICAO) in the technical and safety sectors and a failure in the commercial sphere. The Transit Agreement and the creation of the PICAO are relatively straightforward and will be dealt with first, and then attention will turn to the differences between the British and the Americans and to the differences within the US camp and the failure to achieve a commercial agreement.

The US had many powers and levers to promote its policy preferences: advanced equipment, successful airlines, economic influence and ability to extend or withhold economic aid, and huge prestige as the now-undisputed premier power in the world. In fact, as Britain wanted an agreement on Freedoms 1 and 2 and to establish the ICAO to help standardize technical and safety matters, there was little need for the US to flex its muscles regarding these matters. The ICAO progressed gradually and without great controversy, but there were initial problems with Freedoms 1 and 2. At first they were dealt with in conjunction with commercial Freedoms 3, 4 and 5, and in that context agreement eluded the conference because of the intractable difficulties on commercial rights. It was only when New York Mayor Fiorella LaGuardia of the US delegation and Herbert Symington of the Canadian suggested separating the first two from the last three air freedoms that progress was made. As LaGuardia famously put it, everyone is against bad weather, but they wanted more than weather forecasting and safety provisions. Thereafter things went smoothly. Both countries recognized that Freedoms 1 and 2 were essential to expand services; for example the British needed rights in Hawaii to cross the Pacific.[21] In any event it was the British who proposed the International Transit Agreement composed of Freedoms 1 and 2 and it was widely accepted. The Air Transit Agreement and the establishment of ICAO were the most important achievements of Chicago.[22] The story of Freedoms 3, 4 and 5 was different. Agreement could not be reached, at least not by a sufficient number of states to make it viable.

According to conventional wisdom the Chicago Conference failed to reach accord on rules for commercial operations because of a dispute between Britain and the US over Fifth Freedom rights. The nub of the issue was the extent to which US airlines passing through the UK could pick up passengers in Britain. The British were fearful that extensive Fifth Freedom rights would eat into what they saw as their local market, making UK airlines unviable. The Americans insisted on extensive rights to pick up on through flights as the only way to make long-distance operations commercially viable – impasse followed. Even Churchill and Roosevelt were unable to resolve matters in several lengthy exchanges.[23]

This conventional wisdom is, however, wrong, or at least seriously incomplete. The fact is that key personnel within the US delegation did not want an agreement at Chicago for the automatic exchange of the Five Freedoms because they feared that in the medium to long term that would threaten the viability of US airlines, which in turn would have unacceptable commercial and security consequences. The issue was simply this: either exchange automatically the Five Freedoms multilaterally or negotiate for the exchange of Five Freedoms bilaterally on a state-by-state basis that would allow the US to decide when, with whom and to what extent it thought best to deal on the Five Freedoms. For simplicity's sake the differences within the US administration between the multilateral and the bilateral option will be presented as a tussle between Roosevelt and Pogue.

The first US official civil aviation planning report, which was by a committee chaired and much influenced by Pogue, put matters thus in March 1943:

> As time goes on, our margin of competitive advantage [in post-war international civil aviation] is likely to be reduced. . . . It is not impossible that our situation would remain favorable, but to act on that assumption would involve substantial risks if successful participation in international air commerce is essential to our military security.[24]

Pogue believed it was and that US civilian aviation had to be successful and if that meant forms of protection then so be it. He feared that in the medium term lower foreign labor costs and possible subsidies would eat away at the US's lead in civil aviation. Therefore he strongly committed to a form of protective bilateralism, but one that would nonetheless open the world to a huge expansion of international civil aviation – mainly by US airlines – and one that would be more competitive and efficient: the only caveat was that US airlines must have a leading role in that.

President Roosevelt's attitude was different. In November 1943 he made it very clear what policy he favored. 'Reading from a memorandum which he said he had himself prepared, he gave . . . oral directives.'[25] He declared in favor of 'a very free interchange. That is, he wanted arrangements by which planes of one country could enter any other country for the purpose of discharging traffic of foreign origin, and accepting foreign bound traffic.' He knew what he was talking about. He clearly and precisely explained not only the Third and Fourth Freedoms, but also the Fifth Freedom. Regarding the latter he illustrated what he meant by explaining that a Canadian line operating to Jamaica should be allowed to pick up Fifth Freedom traffic in Buffalo for Jamaica, but not cabotage (internal domestic traffic) traffic for Miami. He was in fact drawing a picture of a general multilateral agreement that would automatically grant transit and stop and commercial outlets in terms of Third, Fourth and Fifth Freedoms to all nations who entered into consort. This was the President's vision of freedom of the air: it was not Pogue's. His view was that:

> With respect to the granting of "commercial outlets" the right of any foreign airline to discharge and take on passengers and traffic, each nation must decide where its best interest lies. It would be quite unrealistic, at this stage of the world's developments, to assume that such commercial outlets should be more or less automatically granted to all comers.[26]

At Chicago according to Pogue's own words regarding the Air Transport Agreement, which incorporated the Five Freedoms: 'I had to sort of play ball because I knew it would fail, but I put forward the transport agreement because that is what Roosevelt commanded us to do.'[27] Pogue later commented that he thought that: 'we had immense advantages that we ought to be taking some credit for and some of these people [who sought a multilateral commercial agreement] were throwing it away I thought.'[28] He believed that Roosevelt was too optimistic: 'We attempted to comply with his wishes . . . but it became clear quite early in the meetings that this Agreement would not be acceptable.'[29] Crucially, Pogue thought that 'the trouble with Roosevelt on aviation was he just didn't know what he was doing.'[30] For those in the US such as Pogue who wanted to negotiate bilaterally for commercial rights, the achievement of the International Air Transit Agreement combined with the ICAO was equivalent to a squaring of the circle.[31] They had the best of all possible worlds. This was the sort of multilateralism that Pogue had always favored. It provided the potential for uniformity of technical and safety provisions through ICAO and the Transit Agreement opened the world to US airlines without the need for tedious bilateral negotiations that would otherwise be required to cross countries to get to major commercial gateways. At the same time the US could use its power and influence to choose bilateral commercial agreements and ensure it only consummated those that would be of benefit to US airlines. For Pogue nothing else was needed from Chicago, except to put in train bilateral commercial negotiations, which the Americans did promptly and robustly. Strong circumstantial evidence suggests that the American delegation, contrary to President Roosevelt's wishes, did not want agreement on a multilateral commercial agreement, which would have automatically delivered commercial rights to all comers for operations into the US.

Detailed accounts of the Chicago story of the Fifth Freedom have been given elsewhere, only the bare bones of what happened is required here.[32] On 12 November the American, Canadian and British delegates hived off from the rest of the conference to try to hammer out a commercial regime. They were in virtual session for two days. According to Berle's account four main points of agreement, or at least near agreement, emerged. There was a compromise on allocation of traffic between national airlines. Initial division of traffic by quotas was to be followed by the application of an escalator whenever load factors were 65% or above and that would enable an airline to launch increased capacity to compete for the growing market. Some in the US delegation thought this was too restrictive, but they also feared that if they did not go down this route then they might have to accept even more restrictive conditions.[33] There were two caveats on the traffic allocation agreement. Firstly, its provisions should not affect established business and traffic flows – something that helped the US where it already dominated markets. Secondly, to protect states disabled in aviation by the war, there was a 'birth-right clause' assigning them traffic for a period of three years after which the normal provisions, namely the escalator, would apply. All this reflected genuine compromise on the part of Britain and the US. Lord Swinton, head of the British delegation, was as reasonably satisfied with this as Berle, head of the US delegation, appeared to be.[34] Furthermore there was movement on agreement about rates with the likely solution being an airline operators' conference making recommendations, subject to government approval. This reflected US views, but was not uncongenial to the British. Thirdly, negotiations had begun on the basis of a Canadian Draft Convention incorporating the Four Freedoms. Berle later explained that the US had argued for the Five Freedoms and that the British had eventually agreed, partly because there was a provision for the Fifth Freedom to be restricted by a price differential: for example a local British service from London to Paris could charge less than Fifth Freedom offerings from a US carrier. This was still an unresolved matter on 14 November and it was not until 16–19 November that attention focused again specifically on the Fifth Freedom. The fourth point concerned strong regulatory power for the international authority. Berle saw this as touchy for both the British and Canadians; however, he pointed out that given agreement on the three preceding points (even though as it transpired the third was in fact far from being resolved) such power became redundant. The authority would have no executive matters with which to deal. According to Berle the British and the Canadians agreed and Stokeley Morgan of the US delegation and Sir Arthur Cribbett of the British were assigned the task of drafting things for presentation to the rest of the conference.[35]

For the fortunes of a multilateral commercial regime, this was the high water mark. But soon the waters of hope ebbed away as controversy erupted again over the Fifth Freedom. After the British accepted provisions for Fifth Freedom traffic the Americans then asked for more on the weekend of 17–19 November and it was that which really caused problems. Part of the background difficulty was that Swinton had accepted an escalator clause – that would allow capacity to be increased in response to high load factors – for Third Freedom traffic on the basis of corrupted instruction from London, which said 'accept the escalator' when in fact, it should have read 'do not accept.'[36] Given the sensitivity of the talks, Swinton felt honor bound to keep to his word with the Americans on escalation for Third Freedom traffic and that was how things stood on 17 November.[37] It looked as if a compromise had actually been agreed on these most difficult of issues. Then on 18 November Berle insisted that the escalator should also apply to Fifth Freedom traffic as well. He and the British had accepted some protection of local traffic by a price differential, which was still hugely difficult for the British, but when the Americans dropped the price differential as well the situation became totally unacceptable.[38] On 21 November one of the Canadian delegates thought that the conference had reached its nadir with Berle withdrawing concessions already agreed. He acknowledged that Swinton was pretty unbending, but 'justification for this position may be found in the US tactics of raising a new demand every time Canada or the UK gave in on a previous demand.'[39] Berle withdrew all reservations supposed to constrain the operation of Fifth Freedoms and was also 'inclined to ask for more and more, including the dropping of the "birth-right" article which was intended to protect liberated areas.'[40] The British made one last concession by suggesting unresolved issues such as the escalator be referred for adjudication by the new international authority, ICAO. As Symington of the Canadian delegation put it: 'By this move the United Kingdom delegation got itself on tenable ground *viz* impartial decision on a disputed matter by an impartial board, and they clung to that position to the end.'[41] At this point Symington approached Pogue to speak to the US delegation about these British proposals in the hope that they 'could well be accepted . . . but he refused saying it was useless.'[42] Not even the entry of President Roosevelt and Prime Minister Churchill into the fray could help: their efforts were to no avail.[43]

At Chicago it was the Americans as much if not more so than the British who scuppered the idea of a multilateral Five Freedoms agreement that would have automatically exchanged the Five Freedoms between all signatories.

Conclusion

There were starkly contrasting views on what Chicago had achieved. The conference chairman Adolph Berle thought: 'The International Conference on Civil Aviation has advanced civil flying by at least twenty years.'[44] In contrast a senior Canadian delegate, J.R. Baldwin, commented: 'We have been in travail for a month and have brought forth a mouse.'[45] Both exaggerated, but what was actually achieved? That question can be answered in two stages. The first in terms of the concrete results – the formal agreements and provisions that the conference produced – and less tangible results in terms of the promise some of those concrete provisions held and the way that the conference raised the profile and expectations of international civil aviation.

The first concrete result of the conference was the International Transit Agreement embodying Freedoms 1 and 2. This was a considerable achievement. No longer would signatories be able to withhold transit and stop provisions or only cede them in return for inflated financial and/or political payments. There were still important countries, which remained outside the Chicago Convention, most notably the Soviet Union, which did not join until 1970, and aviation relations with it remained fraught and highly political throughout the Cold War.[46] Even so, the Transit Agreement opened the world to the possibility of realizing an effective worldwide international aviation passenger system. The other concrete achievement was the ICAO, which was provisional until it came into full force as a specialized agency of the UN on 13 May 1947. Article 44 set out its nine objectives, which can be summarized as promoting safety and the orderly development of civil aviation on a non-discriminatory basis throughout the world. How that broad remit developed will be examined in the next chapter, but it is important to note that this also created a full-time international bureaucracy devoted to the development of worldwide aviation that could rise above parochial state boundaries in its pursuit of international services. In other words this was a possibility for a new voice to arise and speak for the international rather than just the narrow national interest in aviation.

The prospects in at least the less political aspects of international aviation – navigation, safety and uniform technical standards – looked very promising and clear. In contrast, the picture for the commercial side was opaque. The failure to reach agreement on a multilateral commercial regime left the industry dependent upon bilateralism. And there were dangers with this. If matters developed in a repeat of the inter-war period then the future for international aviation looked bleak. As one scholar notes, bilateralism,

> although paying tribute to the sovereign equality of states by putting parties formally on an equal footing, essentially is a power-oriented (rather than a rule oriented) regulatory technique, based on diplomatic *quid pro quo*, horse-trading "carrot-and-stick" or outright economic leverage, which necessarily confers advantages to those states which are in a position to withhold valuable assets and resources from others.[47]

This was the problem: Would the post-war bilateralism operate simply as another form of power politics? Or, would something more progressive emerge?

There were huge pressures for agreements to allow American airlines to consummate the opportunities that had beckoned at Chicago. While the conference failed to create a commercial regime, it had so raised expectations and the profile of aviation that momentum soon carried things forward. There would be no multilateral commercial agreement, but in 1946 the US and Britain struck agreement in Bermuda and created what became known as the Bermuda Model bilateral agreement. And it was on that basis that much of the international civil aviation industry moved forward.

Notes

1 *BNA*, CAB 66, WP(43)257, 22 June 1943, "Post-War Civil Aviation" note by Prime Minister and Minister of Defence, Winston C. Churchill.

2 Other rights, the first two of which later became significant under a more liberal dispensation, are: (vi) the right to pick up 'gateway' passengers in a foreign state and bring them to the airline's country of origin for transfer to another flight with a foreign destination; (vii) the right to commercial carriage between two states, neither of which is the airline's country of origin; and (viii) cabotage.

3 B.B. Berle and T.B. Jacobs (editors), *Navigating the Rapids 1918–71: From the Papers of A.A. Berle*, New York: Brace Jovanovich, 1973, p. 481.

4 See Gavin J. Bailey, *The Arsenal of Democracy: Aircraft Supply and the Anglo-American Alliance 1938–1942*, Edinburgh: Edinburgh University Press, 2013.

5 *FDRL* OF 2955, box 2, folder: CAB 1938, "Proposed Program for Vocational Training in Aviation" undated.

6 See Donald M. Pisano, *To Fill the Skies with Pilots: The Civilian Pilot Training Program 1939–1949*, Urbana: University of Illinois Press, 1993. The British Commonwealth Air Training Plan did something similar for the British Commonwealth, training over 130,000 pilots and crew, and Germany's wartime capabilities in the air were built upon its powerful civil aviation sector.

7 Robert J. Serling, *When the Airlines Went to War*, New York: Kensington Books, 1997, p. 34.

8 *Rowe Papers, FDRL*, box 6, folder: Civil Aeronautics Authority, Confidential Memorandum for Mr. Forrestal, 16 July 1940.

9 For the reasoning behind the claim about British desire to keep close to the Americans see Alan P. Dobson, *Anglo-American Relations in the Twentieth Century: Of Friendship, Conflict, and the Rise and Decline of Superpowers*, London: Routledge, 1995.

10 Some interpret this as hegemonic leadership, but the present author feels that the term 'system' can only be applied in a very loose sense to international aviation because the industry has never been uniform in the character of its operations and thus was never amenable enough to the kind of domination associated with hegemony. In addition at a more theoretical level the author is broadly skeptical of hegemony's explanatory capability: see Alan P. Dobson, 'The USA, Britain and the Question of Hegemony', in Geir Lundestad (editor), *No End to Alliance: The United States and Western Europe, Past, Present and Future*, Basingstoke & New York: Macmillan & St. Martin's, 1998, pp. 134–67.

11 For Canada's role see Alan P. Dobson, 'Flying Between Britain and the USA: Canadian Civil Aviation 1935–1945', *International History Review* 34(4), (December 2012), pp. 655–77; for US policy developments his *FDR and Civil Aviation: Flying Strong, Flying Free*, New York: Palgrave Macmillan, 2011, and for the broader context his *Peaceful Air Warfare: The United States, Britain, and the Politics of International Aviation*, Oxford: Clarendon Press, 1991, chapter 5, and David Devereux, 'British Planning for Post-War Civil Aviation 1942–1945: A Study in Anglo-American Rivalry', *Twentieth Century British History* 2(i), (1991), pp. 26–46.

12 *BNA*, CAB 87/1, RP(41)17, 11 July 1941.

13 *BNA*, CAB 87/1, RP(41)17, 11 July 1941, RP(42)48, 15 December 1942; RP(A) (43)10, 17 March 1943.

14 *BNA*, CAB 87/2, RP(42)48, 'Internationalisation of Civil Aviation after the War, the Finlay Report', 15 December 1942.

15 *CNA*, MG 26 J4 Reel 1472, p. C158782, Memorandum for Prime Minister King, 21 April 1943.

16 *New York Times*, Henry Wallace, 'Freedom of the Air – a Momentous Issue', 27 June 1943; see also J.S. Walker, *Henry A. Wallace and American Foreign Policy*, Westport: Greenwood Press, 1976.

17 *New York Times*, 10 February 1943.

18 *Berle Papers*, FDRL, box 55, folder: Aviation International June–July 1943, Trippe to CAB, 31 May 1943.

19 *Ibid.*, box 54, folder: Aviation International 1942–1943, R.G. Hooker to Berle, 15 June 1943.

20 Samuel Grafton, *New York Post*, 17 November 1944.

21 *FDRL*, FDR PSF, box 93, folder: Subject File Aviation 1944, Berle to FDR 7 December 1944 "International Civil Aviation Conference [Report]", note p. 21.

22 Aviation diplomacy is always complicated. At Chicago, Canada's position was closer to the US than Britain's and so seemed 'more liberal'. It was, but that does not capture the full reality of what was going on. So, for example, contiguous states were exempt in their aviation relationship from the commercial proposals at Chicago and this well suited Canada because it hoped to extract a favourable bilateral agreement from the US because of its strategic geographical position. For similar reasons, it was strongly against the multilateral exchange of transit and technical stop and did not ratify that agreement until *after* it had completed its bilateral agreement with the US.

23 W.F. Kimball, *Churchill and Roosevelt: The Complete Correspondence, 3 volumes*, London: Collins, 1984, November–December 1944 correspondence, volume 3.

24 *Berle Papers*, box 54, folder: Aviation International January–May 1943, Pogue to Berle 2 March 1943, 'Report of the Interdepartmental Sub-Committee on International Civil Aviation' in response to assignment given on 29 January 1943.

25 US National Archives, Washington DC, (hereafter *USNA*), State Department Decimal Files, 800.796/495 memorandum of conversation by Assistant Secretary of State Adolf Berle, 11 November 1943. The President later approved this record of the conversation, see file memorandum 27 December 1943, FDR requested Grace Tully to telephone Berle saying the record was OK, *FDRL FDR PSF*, box 93, folder: Aviation Subject File 1943 Legislation.

26 *Hopkins Papers, FDRL*, box 336, folder: Book 9 Air Conference Post War Aviation, Pogue to Hopkins, 10 November 1943, enclosing draft speech to New York Herald Tribune Forum to be delivered 16 November 1943.

27 Author interview with Welch Pogue, CAB Chairman 1942–1946, 1 August 2000 at the Cosmos Club Washington DC.

28 Pogue Interview.

29 *Ibid.*

30 *Ibid.*

31 Lord Swinton, leader of the British delegation, reserved the position of Newfoundland – a key refueling stop for the northern transatlantic route – until Canada had signed the Two Freedoms Agreement. That caused the Americans some anxiety, thinking Swinton had pulled a fast one, but it all went ahead as planned. *House of Lords Record Office London, Beaverbrook Papers*, box D/248, Dominions Office to Newfoundland 17 January 1945 and extract from Swinton's speech in the House of Lords 16 January 1945. A month later the UK indicated that its signature of the Two Freedoms Agreement should now also be taken to include Newfoundland; see *ibid.* Foreign Office to Washington 5 February 1945.

32 Alan P. Dobson, *FDR and Civil Aviation: Flying Strong, Flying Free*, New York: Palgrave/Macmillan, 2011, chapters 8 and 9.

33 *Berle Papers*, box 216, folder: Diary November–December 1944, memorandum for Under Secretary of State and Interested Offices and Divisions, 14 November 1944.

34 *Beaverbrook Papers*, box D/249, Swinton to Bridges, 13 November 1944.

35 *Berle Papers*, box 216, folder: Diary November–December 1944, memorandum for Under Secretary of State and Interested Offices and Divisions, 14 November 1944.

36 *Ibid.*

37 *Ibid.*, box 216 Berle to Under Secretary of State and Interested Offices and Divisions 26 November 1944; *Howe Papers, CNA*, box 99, folder: Conferences Post war Civil Aviation (19), Baldwin to Howe 25 November 1944 explains discovery of the error; *BNA* CAB 66/56 WP(44)680 memorandum by Cripps refers to escalator clause 'inserted (against our desires) to provide a means of increasing the share of frequencies.'

38 *BNA* CAB 65/44 153(44)2, 22 November 1944; and *Howe Papers*, box 99, folder Conferences-Post War Civil Aviation (19), Baldwin to Howe 21 November 1944.

39 *Howe Papers*, box 99, folder: Post War Civil Aviation (19), Baldwin to Howe 21 November 1944.

40 *Ibid.*

41 *CNA*, RG70 volume 23, Air Canada, folder: TCA 3–3–4 volume 2, Symington to Howe 29 December 1944, enclosing report on the Chicago Conference.

42 *Ibid.*

43 *Berle Papers*, box 216 Berle to Under Secretary of State and Interested Offices and Divisions 14 and 26 November 1944.

44 *Berle Papers*, box 59, folder: ICAC 1944, Berle, Summary 6 December 1944.

45 *Howe Papers*, box 99, folder: Conferences Post-War Civil Aviation (19), Baldwin to Howe 30 November 1944.

46 For an interesting perspective on this see James L. Gormly, 'The Counter Iron Curtain: Crafting an American-Soviet Bloc Civil Aviation Policy 1943–1960', *Diplomatic History* 37(1), (2013), pp. 248–79.

47 Sigmar Stadlmeier, *International Commercial Aviation: From Foreign Policy to Trade in Services*, Paris: Edition Frontiers, 1998, p. 336.

4 The Chicago-Bermuda regime

Its operation and the challenge of deregulation 1945–1992

We . . . believe it desirable to implement without delay our arrangements made at Chicago . . . through bilateral agreements giving us as many gateways to Europe as possible and with no limitation on frequencies.[1]

Introduction: the focus and the challenge

Prospects for crafting a multilateral commercial aviation regime with universal reach were virtually buried at Chicago. They struggled to re-emerge in the shape of the International Air Transport (5 Freedom) Agreement, which entered into force on 8 February 1945, but an insufficient number of states ratified the agreement and its effectiveness has been negligible. Currently only 11 states are party to it and two of those have registered important reservations. ICAO has attempted to resurrect commercial multilateralism from time to time including in Geneva in 1947, Montreal between 23 November and 4 December 1994, shadowing almost exactly the Chicago Conference of 50 years earlier, and again in Montreal in March 2013 and May 2014. In 2013 proposals were tabled for reform of the commercial sector by the New Zealand delegation, but the text seemed pessimistic, almost resigned to failure:

> As the international community has found, most recently at the international trade negotiations at the World Trade Organisation, reaching an international consensus involving many members with a wide range of issues and interests can be particularly challenging.[2]

This is something of an understatement. Commercial multilateralism with universal reach remains elusive, but different roads can lead to multilateralism. One such route opened up with the US turn to Open-skies policy in the 1990s and there have been radical regional developments directly related to the consequences of that, which could provide a springboard for multilateralism. For a long time though, after Chicago, multilateralism was effectively dead in the water.

Confronted with the failure of commercial multilateralism at Chicago the immediate future inevitably lay with bilateralism. The question was: What kind of bilateralism? For a while there were worryingly familiar developments of a predatory and politically aggressive kind, then important developments resulted in a more stable and ordered system structured around the 1946 Anglo-American 'model' ASA, or Bermuda Agreement as it became universally known. While what emerged had wide variations of practice and could not be described as a homogenous system, international aviation expanded hugely between the 1940s and 1970s. Thereafter a confluence of complex developments inaugurated yet another phase of turbulent change triggered by US domestic deregulation leading in 1992 to the US-Netherlands Open-skies agreement, which became the new model bilateral. This presented a challenge to the then-existing dispensation – even in its most liberal guise – and resonates down to the present.

In the first post-war phase for international civil aviation, the Bermuda Model, the ICAO and IATA, the International Transit Agreement and US leadership determined developments. One way of grasping how this worked is by imagining the US at the center with most of the key aviation states revolving like satellites around it and pursuing similar policies, at least in their direct dealings with the US. One should not underestimate the importance of this configuration, as US aviation amounted to approximately 40% of the world's entire market. The satellites however did not always follow the Americans willingly and within their own orbits usually practiced very different policies, as was true during both the Bermuda Model period up until the 1970s and under the more liberal Open-skies Model that followed. Finally, it is also important to mention that the US did not always abide by the principles of the model it urged on others. When US national interest did not coincide with the principles of the Bermuda Model, it followed a different path. So, one must not have the impression that the world aviation market moved forward uniformly under the leadership of the US, the rules and regulations promulgated and nurtured by ICAO and IATA and the International Transit Agreement. It was much better than the inter-war period, but there was still fragmentation, differences in the way standards were applied and above all else there was no level commercial playing field.

What follows is divided into three parts with successive focus on: the Bermuda Model and its operation until 1977; the workings of ICAO and IATA; and finally the US drive for deregulation, which, initially at least, produced an even less homogenous system than under the Bermuda Model. And all that is contained within the improved context agreed at Chicago, namely the International Transit Agreement.

Taming bilateralism? The Bermuda Model 1946–1977

Chicago lifted the profile of civil aviation in such a way that impasse on a commercial regime could not endure. The US was the key to what would happen next, but it had two immediate challenges to meet respectively from Pan Am and Britain.

Pan Am abided as a problem on two counts, the first because it continued to maneuver in order to retain its overseas chosen-instrument/monopoly status. It failed in the end, but it was not a foregone conclusion given the strength of lobbying Trippe could muster in Congress. The second count arose in the aftermath of Pan Am's broken monopoly. American Overseas Airways and TWA were licensed to join Pan Am on transatlantic routes, albeit in separately allocated sectors. Trippe did not take kindly to this and decided to test their mettle. Pan Am reduced its fare from $375 to $275. It was like the old pre-war days of predatory pricing and vicious bilateralism and it was not just US airlines which would be hit by this, but British as well, namely in the shape of the British Overseas Airways Corporation (BOAC), which had succeeded Imperial Airways during the war. As the US ambassador to the Court of St James reported: 'The British Govt. would never permit Panam or any other carrier to fly into England with unlimited frequencies and with unilateral power to set its rates without approval of either IATA or the govt.'[3] So far as Washington was concerned the second proviso of British policy was not a problem: no one wanted a pricing free-for-all. But that meant not just overcoming the discrete problem of Pan Am's present price cut, it meant finding some way of introducing a form of pricing stability across the industry. One way of achieving that was to establish a model bilateral incorporating pricing provisions, which others could be urged to adopt. The leading candidate with whom to conclude such an agreement was Britain, but how to accomplish that after the disputes in Chicago and what followed immediately after was problematical to say the least.

The US wasted no time in moving out into bilateral talks, even engaging with countries during the Chicago Conference. Britain opposed the spread of American routes as best it could but its resources were meagre compared to those of the US and its position soon began to slip.[4] There were many twists in this complicated game of maneuver and countermove, but one of the critical plays came with the US-Eire bilateral signed in early 1945. This was a crucial achievement for the US because it held out the prospect of its airlines bypassing the UK *en route* to Europe. Churchill was furious when he heard about the agreement, writing plaintively to Roosevelt, 'I cannot feel sure that this affair has been brought to your notice' and later implored him 'to have the agreement annulled'. Roosevelt had known all along, had no intention of annulling the agreement and told Churchill so in no uncertain terms, ending: 'I'm sorry but there it is.'[5] The US agreement with Eire was an important part of US strategy to try to push the British into a *modus operandi* that would allow the consummation of their aviation policies. But there was something far more crucial in this scenario and that was Britain's general economic needs. It was those which pushed the British into negotiation with the Americans in early 1946 for an ASA on the island of Bermuda.

In the meantime however important developments intervened. The first and most obvious was Churchill's defeat in the General Election and the coming to power of the Labour government under Prime Minister Clement Attlee. His government was committed to widespread nationalization of British industry and that included civil aviation. Complete nationalization of civil aviation and airports followed in August 1946 with the Civil Aviation Act.[6] In fact government ownership of national carriers was the norm rather than the exception, with the US outstanding as the principal exception. That would continue to be characteristic of the industry until deregulation began to change things in the 1980s. Although nationalized, the immediate aims and priorities for British civil aviation changed little, but those ambitions had to be adjusted in the face of American demands.[7]

The Americans dictated the content of the bilateral air service agreement struck in Bermuda. At the time, Britain was hugely vulnerable to US pressures because of its need for financial assistance. The Anglo-American Loan Agreement had been negotiated and would provide $3.75 billion, but Congress had not yet approved it. That was the main clincher for the Americans who argued that if the British were not to accommodate them in aviation Congress would be unlikely to approve the loan. This was an important lever on the British, who in any case wanted to avoid souring relations with the US for wider security reasons. The crisis came to a head between 4 and 11 February. The head of the British delegation at Bermuda, Lord Winster, wrote to the Cabinet saying:

> If the Cabinet felt that the signing of the agreement was of vital importance from the point of view of our general relations with the United States and the consideration of the loan agreement by Congress, he was willing that our Delegation should be authorised to sign.[8]

The Cabinet was split and it took another week for them to decide, but in the end they authorized Winster to sign.

The Americans were so pleased with what they had extracted from the British that they declared Bermuda a model agreement. This could not replace the homogeneity of multilateralism, but it brought some uniformity and order to the system. Under the Bermuda Model airports had to be designated as international gateways and airlines had to be 'substantially' owned and controlled by either state to an agreement. They were to operate on a basis of 'fair and equal opportunity' through the exchange of Five Freedoms. The Fifth Freedom had been hugely problematic at Chicago, but in Bermuda the US achieved its aims. As the head of the US delegation explained:

> We believe that on frequency control they [the regulatory clauses] now offer no succour to the British concept since it has been made abundantly clear that we do not concede that any regulation is necessary to accomplish a close relationship between services offered and public demand. The Fifth Freedom traffic principles set forth are broad enough to allow an operator to operate satisfactorily and we believe would be violated only if an operator were to go in for really local services, something which the operators have denied they have any desire to do.[9]

The British had tried to prevent 'change of gauge' for US airlines picking up Fifth Freedom traffic, that is to say switching to smaller aircraft for onward flights, but they had even failed to achieve this. US airlines could now freely expand their operations as market demand increased.

Some suggested that there was compromise in the agreement in two key areas – pricing and dispute resolution – but this was hardly the case. On pricing the Americans were as keen as the British to have a system that would deliver stability, though they might present such agreement as a concession to the British for diplomatic reasons. They were more than happy to have prices fixed through IATA tariff conferences. The pricing recommendations coming from these conferences were then routinely approved by governments and in the case of the US granted antitrust immunity.

The most likely area for disputes lay in frequency and capacity issues. Frequency in principle was to be decided unilaterally by each party and capacity was supposed to be liberal, determined by airlines to meet whatever demand arose. This moved away from predetermined capacity levels and only *ex post facto* adjustments were now allowed (i.e. after it could be shown that there was overcapacity or that one side was affecting 'unduly the services' which the other 'provides on all or part of the same routes').[10] In fact, if either government objected to the capacity being flown by the other's airlines, there were all kinds of potential for dispute, which brought in the other area of supposed compromise in the Anglo-American agreement: dispute resolution. Under Bermuda any such disputes could be referred to ICAO for arbitration and decision, but while that seemed something of a victory for the UK and its desire for international regulatory control it was largely Pyrrhic given that the ICAO had no powers of enforcement.

Clearly this more liberal regime was open to interpretation and some analysts believe that any bilateral system has a tendency to conservatism and protectionism.[11] However, the US had such a dominant position in the early post-war years that it was largely able to manipulate matters to be liberal or protectionist as it chose for its own ASAs. Usually when it was a party to a bilateral it extracted liberal provisions for access, frequency and capacity. In such cases the Bermuda Model meant something liberal, but when it suited the US it took a more conservative line in interpreting Bermuda and protected its own market. That was particularly the case for example in negotiations with the Dutch.

The Dutch posed a nightmare scenario for those like Pogue who feared that the US could lose its dominant position if its market were opened to all comers, or even opened to particular countries in the liberal manner of Bermuda as applied to the British. The Netherlands was a problem. It had an effective airline in Koninklijke Luchtvaart Maatschappij (KLM) that could exploit access to the US market, but in return the Netherlands only offered the US access to a tiny domestic Dutch market. Furthermore over the years KLM developed an effective feeder system through garnering Sixth Freedom traffic from other countries within Europe for its services to the US. Combine all that with the possibility of lower operating and labor costs and US airlines were left fearful of a liberal Bermuda-style agreement with the Netherlands and they lobbied accordingly.

In September 1946 during US-Netherlands bilateral talks the Dutch were dismayed that the US would not grant them the four routes they requested, allowing instead only two on temporary licenses. This was particularly ironic as the talks more-or-less coincided with the US-UK negotiations and the Americans declaring that they would follow Bermuda principles in any subsequent ASA. To the Dutch the American position appeared rank hypocrisy after so much talk of liberal access and more market-style operations. They were right: a combination of strategic priorities *and* economic benefits arising from the *status quo* trumped the Bermuda economic principles for the Americans in this case. By any other word this was protectionism. Acting Secretary of State Dean Acheson cabled US Ambassador to the Netherlands Stanley Hornbeck explaining it had never been the US position 'that foreign airlines would automatically be entitled to a multiplicity of routes which could not be justified by actual traffic requirements.'[12] This was simply a reformulation of arguments made repeatedly by Welch Pogue during the run-up to the Chicago Conference when he had opposed President Roosevelt's wishes multilaterally to exchange the Five Freedoms. And the motivation behind Pogue's position was not solely to do with commercial considerations, but extended to broader and long-term security concerns.

Generally ASAs with the US followed a Bermuda-liberal policy, but there were exceptions and, elsewhere when the US was not party to an agreement, the model was often ignored. What happened to Bermuda-type agreements according to one highly experienced airline official was that 'airlines and governments sat down and said whatever this agreement [the Bermuda Model] meant to say we aren't going to let you do more than we want to do.'[13] In Europe this translated into a highly regulated and protected market where foreign routes were generally limited to capital cities, capacity being divided between subsidized state-owned carriers operating under a near-universal single-designation regime (only one airline from each country allowed to operate on the route) and pooling of revenue.

In broad terms one can say that the Chicago International Transit Agreement created worldwide open skies and Bermuda provided the model for how they would generally be commercially exploited. However, within that general framework, there were important anomalies, which can be categorized under three rubrics. The first rubric consists of departures from the liberal spirit of Bermuda by the US, though one needs to recognize that in and of itself the liberal spirit of Bermuda had serious limitations. For a truly liberal market there are many prerequisites, but the three most important are: free route access, free pricing and commercial freedom to determine capacity. Bermuda did not mean liberal or market pricing. It did not mean free entry onto routes. Its liberal elements were solely to do with the ability to expand capacity and increase frequency within a framework liberalized by the International Transit Agreement. Even when interpreted in a liberal spirit, liberalism did not go further than this under the Bermuda Model. The second rubric is that ASAs that did not involve the US were generally much more conservative, as epitomized by the market sharing arrangements in Europe, and this point indicates the limits of US influence in the industry as a whole: it could hardly be described as hegemonic. The fact it dictated the content of the Bermuda Agreement might appear to contradict that judgement, but it was the specifics of the US-UK relationship at the time which empowered the

US and those specifics were eventually to change. By 1977 and the Bermuda 2 Agreement suggestions of US hegemony would seem laughable given that ASA's content. The third rubric, standing largely outside of all this, was one of the biggest aviation nations in the world: the Soviet Union. For our present purposes the Soviet Union is of little interest as it played only a negligible part in the development of the international civil aviation market. It will appear from time to time in what follows, but only as a minor player. However, the point to be made here is that while Chicago, Bermuda, the International Transit Agreement and US leadership overcame much of the negative aspects of inter-war bilateralism and created a more unified operating environment for airlines, there was still fragmentation and major disparities in the way airlines operated in different markets. Eventually after huge growth in the 1950s and 1960s, this new and vastly expanded industry would begin to show major signs of dysfunction. That, combined with operating breakthroughs, technological advances and new economic thinking, introduced deregulation onto the scene and the airlines would go through yet another turbulent period with the new Open-skies Model eventually taking center stage. But before explaining the movement towards that, we must turn to developments in safety, technical standards and the kind of support rendered by IATA to the growth of the airline industry.

ICAO and IATA

Both ICAO and IATA make important contributions for international governance through rules, regulations and practices that dilute the force of anarchy in international affairs. Even for Realists, they are seen as agencies of governance insofar as they are a means for exercising power by sovereign states. IATA may seem an implausible candidate for the exercise of state power, as it is an association of scheduled airlines, but as Chuang has argued, IATA's membership for many years consisted of an overwhelming majority of state-owned airlines and was thus best conceived of as a hybrid non-governmental/inter-governmental organization (NGO/IGO) at least until privatization of airlines gained momentum in the 1980s and 1990s.[14]

The ICAO emerged from the Chicago Convention and it became provisionally operative on 6 June 1945. Its remit was not clearly delineated and at first it attempted to embrace both the economic regulatory side of aviation as well as safety and technical matters. However, as at Chicago, the US opposed commercial regulation by a powerful international body and so ensured that efforts to bring economic regulation under ICAO's authority failed. That meant ICAO would

> develop primarily as a technical organization with a central role in establishing international standards and practices, collecting statistics, and overseeing all the non-economic aspects of international commercial aviation.[15]

This remains largely true in 2017, though ICAO has never completely given up the economic regulatory ghost. In 2014, at a transport symposium in Montreal, the Director of ICAO's Air Transport Bureau, Boubacar Djibo, observed:

> Barriers impede efficiency, generate friction, hinder growth, and lead to a reduction in air transport connectivity.
>
> Whether fragmentation is geographic or economic, or a combination of the two, the barriers posed to an economically sustainable air transport system are inherited from the regulatory framework.[16]

This was all very apt, but simply raised the question posed for 70 years: What to do? Or, more specifically: What can ICAO do? Panelists at the conference voiced support generally for moving away from bilateralism to multilateralism. More specifically:

> Panellists supported going beyond the bilateral paradigm to a multilateral approach – and confronting the fragmentation inherent in the "substantial [national] ownership and effective control" clause found in most bilateral air services agreement.[17]

The delegates knew what needed to be done to create a truly globalized airline system, but they had to square those aspirations with reality, which, as ICAO Council President Olumuyiwa Bernard Aliu explained, amounted to the fact that all ICAO could do was 'work diligently towards consensus at both the global and national levels.'[18] And the reality is that it has never been possible to reach a universal consensus for multilateral regulation in the commercial aviation sphere. Such reality intruded into the negotiations for the 2007 EU-US Air Transport Agreement, when the US insisted on retaining 'substantial ownership and effective control' of US airlines. It was the stumbling block that prevented the creation of a common transatlantic aviation area with common ownership rules for airlines and meant that the Gordian knot tying the operation of airlines into a system of national sovereign airspace was only loosened and not untied.

ICAO has played no significant role in the development of the commercial side of the international aviation system except indirectly by its development of safety and technical standards and the support it has given to infrastructure developments, especially navigational. In those areas, it has had huge impact.

At the heart of ICAO's work are SARPs: standards and recommended practices. Through these ICAO strives to develop a standardized and safe operating environment for international civil aviation and it has to do this by argument and appeal to a common-sense desire among all aviation states for safe and secure airline travel. In addition ICAO has used its meagre resources in conjunction with the UN Development Programme (UNDP) to help poorer states develop infrastructure and meet safety standards. Such help has been important, though in the great scope of things it needs to be placed in context: ICAO's total annual budget in the mid-1980s was about $130 million and total assistance from ICAO and UNDP peaked in 1982 at just under $65 million, which would not cover the cost of one Boeing 747.[19] Most countries had to pay their own way. Even so the airlines soon began to thrive. Passenger numbers rose 40% between 1945 and 1946 and were nine times the pre-war level, though one needs to remember that this was from a very small base number. ICAO's first President, Edward Warner was able to explain in 1950 just how much advance had been achieved after only four years of existence:

> Aircraft over most of the earth are already flown in accordance with ICAO's Rules of the Air. Their personnel are beginning to be licensed to ICAO's standards. Their pilots are briefed before flight by the use of NOTAMs [Notices to Airmen] prepared and transmitted in accordance with an ICAO-shaped pattern. The meteorological forecasts given are drawn to an ICAO specification. After the flight begins, communication between aircraft and the ground is conducted in ICAO-adopted codes and in ICAO-specified phraseology. The pilot makes his instrument approach, if an instrument approach be necessary, on an ILS [instrument landing system] of which the characteristics have been standardized by ICAO to assure the closest possible uniformity of approach path and of character of instrumental indication at aerodromes throughout the world. The charts of the country over which he flies, and the large-scale chart that shows surroundings of the airport at which he is to land and the standard method of approaching it, have their size, color scheme and the meaning of their symbols determined by an ICAO standard.[20]

And all this, and much more as time went by, was achieved without ICAO having the power to coerce its members. At most it could suspend their voting rights (often done as a penalty for failing to pay dues) and/or embarrass members by publicizing matters and effectively appealing to the power of international opinion.

The nature of ICAO, an inter-governmental organization where national representatives safeguard their respective countries' national interests, means that when politics intrudes, matters become fraught and outcomes difficult to achieve, whereas in non-politically charged areas of activity it can play a hugely constructive role. Sources of political intrusion have included ostracism of Spain after the war for its ties with the Axis, Cold War friction, the Arab-Israeli conflict, apartheid in South Africa, Portugal's colonialism and later, and more complicated, the response to terrorism. ICAO has had some notable successes even in difficult political contexts. For example in the 1952–1953 dispute between India and Pakistan, over India's direct air route across Pakistan to Afghanistan, it played an important mediatory role, which resulted in a satisfactory compromise giving India designated corridors into Afghanistan. But such successes are few and far between; as one scholar observed, ICAO 'has had limited success when parties concerned are willing to let ICAO help. . . . In matters in which the dispute over civil aviation is only one small part of a larger quarrel, the council can do little.'[21]

Being able to achieve objectives in ICAO in the face of politicized circumstances even eluded the US. Effectively ICAO simply needs to remain passive to veto change. There has to be a strong consensus for action and that was not the case when the US called for extradition rights in the face of a spate of hijackings in the 1970s. When those demands failed it advocated sanctions, but its efforts once again proved bootless. ICAO instead turned its attention to the less politically charged business of implementing preventative measures, where it achieved notable successes.

There are very clear limits circumscribing ICAO's ability to act in political areas, except on those rare occasions where a consensus can be formed. Having said that, one should not underestimate the progress that ICAO achieved in improving security at airports and on airlines in the wake of terrorist atrocities. Furthermore, the response to terrorism led ICAO into a new area of activity: oversight of implementation.

Terrorism galvanized ICAO into action in the field of security. 'Without the same degree of political division [as the UN] . . . ICAO was well suited to negotiate international instruments to enhance aviation security.'[22] And it did: the Tokyo, Hague and Montreal Conventions, the Montreal Protocol and Convention on Plastic Explosives (concerned with the marking and forensic tracking of the source of explosives), Annex 17, which was periodically updated and which set security standards, and the production of the Security Manual to disseminate best practice. However, it was one thing to promulgate standards, another to implement them and it soon became apparent that there were huge discrepancies in the way different countries applied them. As a result in 1989 ICAO took steps, in conjunction with the UNDP, to assess implementation effectiveness:

> The most notable and far-reaching element of the program was the voluntary and confidential evaluation of members' security policies undertaken by ICAO personnel. ICAO was moving into an area that had previously been left to the members themselves – overseeing the implementation of standards and procedures.[23]

This oversight power was desperately needed to publicize and embarrass states into some form of compliance. In 1994 after over 100 evaluations it was found that not a single country was in full compliance with the strictures of Annex 17. ICAO's role continued to develop in this sphere, most notably with the Council approving the establishment of the Universal Safety Oversight Audit Programme, which came into operation in 1998 and since 2008 operates alongside IATA's Operational Safety Audit.[24] ICAO's Strategic Action Plan that same year also emphasized the importance of oversight of implementation and maintenance of standards. In the aftermath of 9/11, ICAO created the Universal Security Audit Programme as a counterpart to the Safety Audit and in July 2002 established the Aviation Security Bureau. ICAO was now not only the main source of generating technical and safety standards, it played a major role in oversight which had direct bearing on implementation.

Since the 1970s ICAO has also become involved in environmental issues, partly prompted by the noise pollution problem posed by Concorde. In 1983 it established the Committee on Aviation Environmental Protection and has played significant roles across the spectrum of environmental concerns, holding conferences, disseminating information and establishing targets and standards. On noise pollution it has set decreasing noise levels for chapter 3 and 4 type aircraft (chapter 2 are no longer allowed in the EU). All aircraft manufactured after 2006 must meet chapter 4 specifications. The US and the EU (and others) may apply even stricter standards than those promulgated by ICAO, but the latter provides the benchmarks for universal application. These developments were helpful, but as we shall see in the conclusion, the problem of pollution not only abides, but continually compounds. In addition to its activities on pollution ICAO also found itself playing a part in resolving the thorny issue of carrier liability, which arose within the Warsaw Convention as a result largely of US refusal to accept low liability cover, but this was resolved more because of initiatives taken by IATA, to which attention must now be turned.

The Havana Conference of major scheduled airlines composed the articles of association for IATA in April 1945 and it was incorporated into law by an act of the Canadian Parliament in December 1945. Its headquarters are in Montreal, the same city that is home to the ICAO. By 2014 it had about 230 member airlines and they were responsible for approximately 93% of scheduled services. IATA's remit is:

> to promote safe, regular and economical air transport for the benefit of the peoples of the world; to foster air commerce and to study the problems connected therewith, to provide the means for collaboration among the air transport enterprises engaged directly or indirectly in international air transport services; and to cooperate with ICAO and other international organizations.[25]

Over the years IATA has performed important support services for the industry including facilitating interlining, standardization of ticketing, data collection and financial settlements between actors in the industry currently through the worldwide Billing and Settlement Plan and Cargo Accounts Settlement Systems. It has also acted as a lobbyist for the industry, promoting its profile and arguing for changes; for example it was the 1995 IATA Conference in Washington, DC, which established a two-tier liability agreement which finally resolved the problems with the Warsaw Convention. The agreement provided for strict liability up to a specified level (acceptable to the US), but anything over that carriers could try to prove absence of liability.[26] This arrangement was subsequently adopted by ICAO and formed the basis for the Montreal Convention of 1999. However, IATA's primary role for much of the period since its inception has been as the agent for coordinating (fixing) rates in the industry, subject to government approval and in the cases of the US and later the EU accompanied by the granting of antitrust immunity.

For many, the stabilization of prices was most welcome and it meant the avoidance of predatory pricing, at least of the obvious and vicious kind.[27] Only rarely were there problems before the mid-1970s. The most celebrated exception was the Chandler, Arizona, IATA Rate Conference of 1962. There the airlines agreed to raise transatlantic return fares by $27, but the market-oriented chairman of the US CAB, Alan Boyd, refused to approve them and a crisis of no small proportion ensued with, among other things, the British government demanding TWA impose the new fares for flights into London. When it did not do so the British authorities collected $27 from arriving passengers and handed the money over to TWA. In the end the US authorities backed down, but the whole episode was an augury of things to come.

In 1978 in the midst of moves to deregulate the US domestic airline industry, CAB Chairman Alfred Kahn issued a Show Cause Order (SCO) requiring that good reason be shown why IATA rates should be given antitrust immunity in the US. This was the beginning of the gradual erosion of IATA's domination of fare setting internationally. It is a long story and not yet fully played out, but in 2006 the European Commission issued a regulation ending antitrust immunity for IATA price fixing in the EU as of 1 January 2007.[28] The Competition Commissioner Neelie Kroes explained that:

> IATA passenger tariff conferences appear to facilitate interlining on routes to third countries, but I do not have sufficient assurances that they continue to benefit passengers on journeys within the EU. The possible prolongation beyond 2007 of the exemption for tariff conferences on routes to non-EU countries depends on the provision of data showing that IATA interlining continues to benefit consumers.[29]

Sufficient evidence was not forthcoming that it did and the EU revoked antitrust immunity in 2007: the US did likewise for transatlantic and Australian routes. As one scholar commented:

> the upsurge in flexible fare setting and US/EC Air Transport Agreement of 2007 with its cooperative agenda for antitrust enforcement, IATA's durability as a tariff-setting force in the international air transport economic order is likely in terminal decline.[30]

Whether or not that is the case remains to be seen. IATA has proved very resilient over the years, but it has clearly lost its central role in fare setting that it had before 1978.

These surveys of ICAO and IATA have moved chronologically ahead of the main account for two reasons. The first reason is that, apart from IATA fare conferences, the contributions of ICAO and IATA have proven to be largely uncontroversial and delivered through well-established procedures and conventions. They provide a relatively stable backcloth to the more politically difficult changes that have taken place in the commercial operations of the airlines. This is not to ignore the facts that there have been important changes in IATA and ICAO. The latter for example has expanded in membership and thus become ever more subject to political intrusions, its size now makes it more difficult to manage and get things done and the days of the large aviation nations leading and determining policy are long gone. However, these changes have not had major impact on the overall character of the international civil aviation industry and the way it operates. Hence the overview offered in this section provides a stable backdrop for what is to come in the commercial sector. The second reason is because, again with the caveat of IATA rate conferences, these two institutions developed under different dynamics than those pushing the development of the broader industry along. They essentially deal with functional non-political issues, or political issues about which it is relatively easy to form a consensus. Both ICAO and IATA will reappear from time to time in the chapters that follow, but the main things to say about them have been said apart from some concluding remarks.

Of the two ICAO has been by far the most important contributor to the development of the industry. It has developed in terms of capabilities and expertise over the years, but it is still clearly an inter-governmental organization with few signs or examples of its members acting in a manner that transcends national loyalties.

It is first and foremost an inter-governmental organization where members represent the interests of their country and its airlines, but ICAO's great achievement has been consistently to create a series of SARPs that sit in a political no-man's land, which allows consensus to emerge. ICAO even managed to do this in the difficult area of security, with the US and Europe taking the lead. ICAO security standards now set the benchmark for all to follow, though the US and Europe also still apply their own unilaterally or bilaterally agreed standards in some cases. The executive leadership arm of ICAO, the Council, has no power to force members to do anything that they really do not want to do. When the Council attempts to move beyond that position outcomes are not predictable and usually they become entangled in politics and fail to be accepted: inaction is tantamount to veto in ICAO. The trick is to demonstrate that SARPs are to the benefit of the industry as a whole and to all the Member States.

IATA has also had to operate on the basis of consensus. In doing so it has been highly successful in technical and non-political arenas, some of which (such as safety) overlap and supplement the work of ICAO. However, and somewhat unlike ICAO, right from the outset IATA took upon itself a potentially highly political role, namely fare coordination. In the light of inter-war experience there was a widespread consensus, that also embraced the US, that the industry should avoid predatory and unfair pricing. That consensus held with only one major exception – the Chandler rates conference – until the mid-1970s. Then the US began to break away and pursue the goal of more competitive pricing. Unlike the situation in ICAO, the US had a major ally in its pursuit of more competitive fares: market forces and later other countries, the first of which was the Netherlands. As a result IATA began to lose its grip on one of its most important and characteristic functions. The kind of veto that operated in ICAO to block US attempts to introduce extradition powers and sanctions was not effective in the long run in IATA.

Like ICAO, IATA has also changed in character over the years. When Chuang did his study of IATA in the early 1970s, it sounded plausible to describe the organization as an hybrid inter-governmental because of all the state-owned air-lines that were members and thus directly answerable to their governments and as non-governmental because it consisted of an association of airlines, some of which at least were privately owned corporations.[31] Over the years however the balance has shifted dramatically, with more and more airlines undergoing privati-zation in the wake of deregulation, and IATA is now much more of a conventional NGO. This has increased the possibility of an international bureaucracy evolving which has a prime loyalty to the international airline industry rather than to a mul-tiplicity of nation states. Just how far that has evolved is difficult to say. However, even if one were to accept its fully fledged existence, its power and influence has clear limitations when measured against the power of individual states such as the US or organizations such as the Commission of the EU. Some have seen the supra-nationalist hand of IATA at work in the way the industry has been re-crafted over the last five decades, but its impact in terms of promoting regime-changing policies seems to have been rather peripheral. After all IATA has been powerless to prevent its role of rate coordination being largely stripped away by the US and the EU.

For those interested in the generics of international governance the experience of ICAO and IATA have much of interest to say.

Liberalization and deregulation 1977–1992

For thirty years the US remained more-or-less content with the regime it had done so much to construct around the Air Transit Agreement and Bermuda and the work of ICAO and IATA. Then in the 1970s new and more radical ideas arose. They came at the very time that the aviation industry needed new thinking because of the economic disaster that hit it in the aftermath of the Yom Kippur War and the astronomical rise in oil prices orchestrated by the Organization of Petroleum Exporting Countries (OPEC). The industry nose-dived. In 1974 13 carriers oper-ating with Boeing 747s flew the equivalent of 25 out of every 51 of them empty across the north Atlantic. That was not sustainable. Something had to change.[32]

Just as economic problems buffeted the industry, new technology and new economic thinking opened new possibilities. However, technology from one per-spective seemed part of the problem because it delivered greater capacity *via* the jumbo-jet at the very time that demand ebbed dramatically away. There were fewer and fewer passengers to fill the vastly increased number of seats. Even so, from a broader perspective, it eventually became clear that the jumbo-jet, the develop-ment of computer reservation systems (CRSs) that could cope with an enlarged and vastly complicated market, new economic theory and political action would transform the industry and lead it to new heights of success and expansion.

The new economic theory that was emerging came mainly from the Chicago School in the USA and it challenged the conventional wisdom of Keynesianism and the idea that regulating industries, such as civil aviation, was necessary for public and consumer interests.[33] The newly discovered Laffer Curve predicted macroeconomic benefits through lower taxes and that – along with privatization, deregulation and the supply-side revolution – framed the dominant position of economic thinking. Those economic ideas gained purchase in mainline politics in the US and led on to dramatic changes. No one really knew what the net effects on a large airline market would be if it were to be deregulated, but once Jimmy Carter became president in 1977 people soon found out.[34]

President Ford and high-profile Senate hearings chaired by Senator Edward Kennedy eased the way forward for Carter in reforming the domestic US airline industry. Kennedy on one occasion pithily responded to a woman's complaint that she had never been able to fly: 'That's why I'm having the hearings.'[35] The groundwork was well prepared and in his first message to Congress on 4 March 1977 President Carter announced:

> One of my Administration's major goals is to free the American people from the burden of over-regulation. As a first step toward our shared goal of a more efficient less burdensome Federal government, I urge the Congress to reduce Federal regulation of the domestic commercial airline industry.[36]

It took nearly two years before the 1978 Airline Deregulation Act became law, but when it did its effects reverberated across the Atlantic and around the world. Its impact grew both because of further political action taken by the US and because of market dynamics which came into play, released by the first phase of US domestic deregulation. Competitive forces began to seep into the international terrain just as the Carter administration turned its attention to developing strategy for dealing with the overseas marketplace. The 1978 US government policy statement declared its guiding principles would be

> to trade competitive opportunities, rather than restrictions, with our negotiating partners. We will aggressively pursue our interests in expanding air transportation and reduced prices rather than accept the self-defeating accommodation of protectionism. Our concessions in negotiations will be given in return for progress toward competitive objectives, and those concessions themselves will be of a liberalising character.[37]

Some of this was so liberal that it seemed like folly to America's established international carriers such as Pan Am and TWA, Partly because of these companies' lobbying and partly because of broader political concerns, members of Congress passed the International Air Transportation Competition Act in 1979 to try to rein in the Administration and ensure that ASAs were more clearly in America's immediate interests. The Congress placed more emphasis on equal benefits and trying to ensure that infatuation with liberalization did not blind the US Department of Transport and the Carter Administration to the danger of imbalances in ASAs. The act specified that the USA should only grant access to the US market in return for 'benefits of a similar magnitude for US carriers.'[38]

Even so, with some temporary exceptions, liberal ASAs became the hallmark of US international aviation and gradually morphed into what we know today as Open-skies policy. By 1980 a dozen liberal bilaterals had been negotiated and, while most were with fairly insignificant players, agreements with Holland, Belgium and West Germany, all concluded in 1978, were to have important consequences for spreading competition and stimulating change in the sclerotic European aviation market. This was the first and most enduring of American strategies to deregulate the international marketplace; the second was Kahn's SCO.

On 9 June 1978 the CAB suggested that IATA fare setting might not be in the public interest and thus not warrant antitrust immunity. It issued a SCO requiring IATA to justify its current practices. This provoked international outrage. It was seen as the worst type of American unilateralism and an attempt by the CAB to stop inter-airline fare agreements and destroy IATA, or at least IATA in its role as a fare coordinator.[39] The SCO did not destroy IATA, but over the following years its fare-setting role was increasingly diminished and the SCO specifically helped to push the Europeans into a more competitive transatlantic price regime in 1982, negotiated under the auspices of the European Civil Aviation Conference (ECAC) and the US State and Transportation Departments.[40] Regulation was beginning to give way to some price competition.[41]

Acting in tandem with US liberalization strategies ran market forces, some preceding the legal and institutional moves for reform, others released and nurtured by them. The conventional wisdom was that economies of scale could not be reaped by airlines. An airline could get bigger and possibly make more overall profit, but on a *pro rata* basis profit margins would remain constant, or more likely would decline as larger operations meant more management difficulties. These assumptions were about to be destroyed.

> What was discovered were economies of scale . . . i.e. you organised your system in such a way that you were able to consolidate large amounts of traffic at a point and then redistribute that traffic. For each unit . . . that you flew, if you had . . . higher load factors on that piece of equipment in effect you had a more productive piece of equipment – a more productive unit of production.[42]

This was the hub-and-spoke configuration of routes. Prior to deregulation, load factors over the previous decade had averaged 52%. In the six years following deregulation it averaged about 59%. More importantly, when demand was depressed post-deregulation, load factors were over 10% higher than in similar periods pre-deregulation.[43] And these load factors were with vastly expanded passenger numbers. Inhibitions about expansion were now replaced by enthusiasm for more economies of scale, more hubs and spokes, and more profits. As US government policy pursued liberal bilateral ASAs, which opened up more and more US international gateways based on the old domestic carriers' hubs, American Airlines (AA), United Airlines (UA) and Delta carried all before them. Well positioned through their inter-connected hubs and their vast number of feeder spokes to assemble large numbers of domestic US passengers, there seemed an irresistible logic that the traditional domestic operators should now use their dominance over the internal US market to thrust out their spokes into the international sphere and that is precisely what they did. However, one should also note that this would not have been possible without CRSs to cope with the increase in passengers and greater complexity in routing them. By the mid-1980s the major CRSs could 'juggle one hundred million fares at a single time.'[44] These changes destroyed traditional overseas carriers, such as Pan Am and TWA, which did not have well-developed US domestic networks to feed passengers into their international gateways.

All of a sudden the civil aviation system was changing rapidly and newly unleashed competition was having a major impact. Among other things this unsettled many airlines and some governments in Europe and prompted more intense thinking there about liberalization.[45] John Steele, the European Commission's Transport Director General from 1981 to 1986, believed that the beginning of reform in Europe 'was a reaction to events in the USA and the realisation that the same concerns existed in Europe and that unless the system was made more flexible it would break.'[46] As one senior US airline executive put it, the choice in Europe was between providing ever-larger subsidies for, usually, state-owned airlines, or changing to run with the market direction flowing from the US.[47]

However, the US was not dominant enough to achieve immediately what it aimed for: in the face of virulent opposition it decided it would be prudent to back down and withdraw the SCO. Equally importantly its policies suffered a huge setback in the negotiations for a new ASA with Britain during 1976–1977. In London, in the midst of recession, the liberal cast of Bermuda became part of the industry's problem so far as the British were concerned. It had resulted in close on a 60–40% split in the US-UK market in favor of US airlines by the mid-1970s. For Edmund Dell, the British minister in charge of aviation, that meant loss of overseas earnings, which were so vital in Britain's precarious economic circumstances. The situation was deemed intolerable and the British renounced the agreement in 1976 in order to seek a more regulated market.[48] This was at the very time that the US looked not to regulate the market further, but just the opposite – to deregulate it. In any event Bermuda 2 was a disaster for the US. They were outmaneuvered and out-negotiated. The US lost many of its Fifth Freedom rights, it was cut back to two double designation routes, capacity now had to be agreed at the start of each operating year and not *ex post facto* as in Bermuda 1, and more routes into the US were opened up for British airlines.[49] But that was not the worst of it for the US.

Specific difficulties arose in the aftermath of Bermuda 2 and led on to an even more costly reversal of US liberalization policies. In early retrospect the Americans regretted much of what was agreed in Bermuda 2 and almost immediately began to complain about the loss of double designation on the Boston to London route. The political clout in Washington from Boston's home state was such that remedial moves soon developed as a result of lobbying on the Carter Administration from Tip O'Neil, Leader of the House of Representatives, and Senator Edward Kennedy, both from Massachusetts. Bermuda 2 was duly amended in 1980 and, among other things, double designation returned to Boston. In return, as part payment however, the American delegation bought into the Traffic Distribution Rules (TDRs) for London airports that had been introduced by Dell in 1977.[50] These, in particular, sought to restrict access to Heathrow to prevent over-congestion. Later, the more cynical and/or perceptive thought they were designed to limit competition with British Airways (BA) and its main operations out of Heathrow. The US-UK ASA now stipulated that:

> Any London airport (including Heathrow) may be served by British Airways, Pan American World Airways and Trans World Airlines (or their corporate successor airline in any name change, merger, acquisition or consolidation in which any of the above three airlines is the major element).[51]

As Cyril Murphy of United Airlines put it in the 1990s: 'it blows my mind . . . the most important international airport in the world and the US is limited to two carriers.'[52] Most American officials were appalled at what they had done. Bermuda 2 was a model of how they now thought the international civil aviation market should NOT work.

> Every city pair is restricted in terms of entry. Every city pair market is restricted in terms of capacity. Every city pair is restricted in terms of fares the airlines may charge passengers. There is no aspect of the market that is not being regulated pursuant to UK insistence.[53]

Over the following years, US-restricted access to Heathrow became the greatest anomaly in the growth of the US's expanding array of Open-skies agreements: it was also their prime target for change.

This is not to say that there were not doubts and hesitations about deregulation in the US and opposition from its established international carriers and protectionist segments of the US Congress. Even the Reagan administration was initially cautious, but the changes that reform had brought about seemed overwhelmingly positive. By 1990 US airlines carried twice as many international passengers as they had done in 1980, increasing their market share by 20%, routes proliferated, capacity and frequency grew apace and prices went down.[54] By the early 1990s it now seemed right to capitalize on these gains and renew the drive for even more liberalization. Open-skies soon became the paradigm for the US and later for much of Europe, but much had to happen in the industry before that and it had to endure the catastrophic fall-out from the First Gulf War.

Conclusion

The international civil aviation industry travelled a huge distance on its development path between the mid-1940s and the early 1990s. The regime that emerged after the war would not have been possible without the central role of the US, but it is important to note that it could not dictate every aspect of the way the industry operated. It set the dominant tone and that was the more liberal regime of the International Transit Agreement and Bermuda working in tandem. It was also a more orderly system than the inter-war one and that was partly to do with the work of ICAO and IATA, which together oiled the technical, safety, security, navigational and day-to-day workings of the airlines often in such mundane but nevertheless essential ways, as standard ticketing.

The commercial operations of the industry were generally much less dysfunctional than they had been before the war, but they were by no means uniform and there was no level commercial playing field. Bermuda was a useful model, but its application varied and in many cases it was not applied at all. After Bermuda 2 was negotiated, the Anglo-American ASA was no longer the model to follow, but the model to avoid if the new liberal dispensation promoted by the US were to succeed. The international aviation industry in the early 1990s stood on the edge of much confrontation and such radical changes that would turn out to be comparable in their impact to that of the International Transit Agreement, Bermuda Model and developments in ICAO and IATA between 1945 and the 1990s. And in many ways the most radical changes wrought were in what had been a highly conservative and tightly regulated market: Europe's.

At Chicago the idea of multilateral worldwide regimes for the three components of the industry were tabled as opportunities. The first dealt with safety and technical provisions, the second with innocent passage and technical stop and the third with the commercial sector in terms of Freedoms 3, 4 and 5. If all three had been achieved then there would have been the real possibility of a truly globalized international civil aviation industry. That does not mean an industry simply characterized by free market operations. It is doubtful if that were ever possible given the nature of the beast: the safety and public service requirements; airlines as symbols of national identity and promoters of national interest; and their relationship to national security through their up-lift capabilities and the wider implications for aerospace manufacturing and research and development. Even so these factors do not deny the possibility of some form of effective globalization. It would not look the same as for some other industries, but would have the same essentials such as globally harmonized competition rules, universal rules for investment and ownership and global standards for safety, security and technical standards. Such principles would not pre-empt caveats to safeguard national security interests, such as the US Civil Reserve Air Fleet (CRAF), which allows the US government in times of crisis to call upon US civil airlines for up-lift capacity to transport troops abroad (more of this in Chapter 6). As argued at the outset of this study a 'globalized international civil aviation industry' means the idea of a level playing field run in principle on any kind of basis, including one far from the ideal of a free and competitive market. The only overriding principle is that all players act in accordance with the same rules and regulations.

If the above argument is compelling, or even plausible, then developments in Europe and particularly the development of the SEAM have two important reasons for attention. Firstly, the SEAM created within the EU a regionalized version of the globalized vision presented above. Secondly, the SEAM took form in parallel with growing ambitions that something like this could be used to create a critical mass that would attract and draw in the rest of the world and regionalization would thereby morph into globalization. And the best way forward with that would be an agreement between the EU and the US to create a common transatlantic aviation area. These are the broad concerns that underlay the next two chapters.

Notes

1 *USNA*, State Department decimal file 811.79641D/1–2945, Acting Secretary of State, Joseph Grew to US Delegation, Dublin, 29 January 1945.
2 ICAO online archive, Worldwide Air Transport Conference 6th Meeting Montreal 18–22 March 2013, AT Conf/6-WP/34, 'Multilateral Agreement on Liberalization of International Air Transportation: A Basis for the Future Economic Regulation of Air Services', proposed by New Zealand Delegation. Interestingly at the ICAO meeting to commemorate the 70th anniversary of the Chicago Conference the Council passed an extraordinary resolution, but it made no mention of a multilateral economic regime for aviation, while affirming the principles and aims of the Chicago Convention. See appendix 1 and comments in the next section.
3 *USNA*, State Department decimal file 711.4127/11–2445, John Winant to Secretary of State 24 November 1945.
4 See Alan P. Dobson, *Peaceful Air Warfare: The United States, Britain, and the Politics of International Aviation*, Oxford: Clarendon Press, 1991, pp. 177–88.
5 Churchill to Roosevelt 27 January and 6 March and his reply 15 March 1945 in Kimball *Churchill and Roosevelt*, pp. 519–20 and 566–7.
6 *BNA*, CAB 21/2229, Cmd. 6712, December 1945.
7 David R. Devereux, 'State versus Private Ownership: The Conservative Governments and British Civil Aviation 1951–62', *Albion*, 27(i), 1995, pp. 65–85.
8 *BNA*, CAB 128/5, 11(46)8, 4 February 1946, memorandum by Lord Winster CP37(46).
9 *USNA*, State Department decimal files: 841.796/1–2746, George P. Baker to Under Secretary of State for Economic Affairs, Clayton, 27 January 1946.
10 Cmd. 6747, *US, UK, Civil Air Services Agreement Bermuda*, 1946, Bermuda Final Act Article 9.
11 *Ibid.*; H.A. Wassenbergh and H.P. van Fenema (editors), *International Air Transport: A Legal Analysis*, Deventer, Kluwer, 1981.
12 *USNR*, RG 197 CAB, BIAND, IAAN, box 62, folder "Netherlands 1943–1947"; Dean Acheson, Acting Secretary of State to US Embassy in the Netherlands, October 26, 1946, see Giles Scott-Smith and David J. Snyder, 'A Test of Sentiments: Civil Aviation Politics and the KLM Challenge in Dutch-American Relations', *Diplomatic History* 37(v), (2013), pp. 917–45.
13 Author interview with Robert Ebdon, Head of Government Affairs, British Airways, 5 August 1991.
14 Chuang, *International Air Transport Association*.
15 David Mackenzie, *ICAO: A History of the International Civil Aviation Organization*, Toronto: Toronto University Press, 2010, p. 127.
16 Djibo speaking at the Air Transport Development: Setting the Course, 2nd ICAO Air Transport Symposium, May 2014 Montreal, *ICAO Journal* 69(iii), (2014), p. 33.
17 *Ibid.*, p. 34.
18 *Ibid.*, p. 3, Presidential address.
19 Eugene Sochor, 'International Civil Aviation and the Third World: How Fair Is the System?', *Third World Quarterly* 10(iii), (1988), pp. 1300–22, at p. 1317.
20 Quoted from Mackenzie, *ICAO*, p. 174, source Edward Warner, 'ICAO after Four Years', *Air Affairs* 3(2), (1950), pp. 281–97, at pp. 281–2.
21 Mackenzie, *ICAO*, p. 202.
22 *Ibid.*, p. 329.

23 *Ibid.*, p. 341.
24 *IATA website, Operational Safety Audit*: 'The total accident rate for IOSA carriers in 2013 was 2.5 times lower than the rate for non-IOSA operators. As such, IOSA has become a global standard, recognized well beyond IATA membership. As of October 2014, 154 (38%) of the 402 airlines on the IOSA registry were non-IATA member airlines.' www.IATA.org.
25 *Act of Incorporation, Articles of Association, Rules and Regulations*, IATA 9th Publication: Montreal, IATA, 1967, Article iii.
26 A strict liability limit of 100,000 Special Drawing Rights was originally set: see Diedericks-Verschoor, *Air Law*, chapter 4.
27 In the 1980s Freddie Laker alleged Laker Airways was put out of business by predatory pricing by British Airways, Pan Am, TWA, et al. Eventually, there was an out-of-court settlement for $50 million.
28 Regulation (EC) No. 1459/2006, 28 September 2006.
29 European Commission Press Release Database, 8 October 2006.
30 Brian F. Havel, *Beyond Open Skies: A New Regime for International Aviation*, The Netherlands: Kluwer International Law, 2009, p. 226.
31 Chuang, *IATA*. In the early 1970s out of 92 active members of IATA 56 were either fully or majority owned by governments and only 24 were fully private. But liberalization changed that in the 1980s and 1990s: 'As a result the vast majority of the members of IATA today are privately owned, privately controlled airlines.' Ludwig Weber, 'International Organizations', in Elmar Maria Giemulla and Ludwig Weber (editors), *International and EU Aviation Law: Selected Issues*, The Netherlands: Kluwer Law International, 2013, pp. 75–129 at p. 119.
32 Alan P. Dobson, *Flying in the Face of Competition: The Policies and Diplomacy of Airline Regulatory Reform in Britain, the USA and the European Community 1968–94*, Aldershot: Avebury Press, 1995, chapter 4.
33 M. Feldstein, 'The Retreat from Keynesian Economics', *The Public Interest* (Summer 1981), pp. 92–105.
34 See Dobson, *Flying in the Face of Competition*. Commercial airline deregulation *within* states such as California provided a clear indication for some as to what would happen; for example Alfred Kahn.
35 Stephen G. Breyer, 'Working on the Staff of Senator Ted Kennedy', *Legislation and Public Policy* 14, (2011), p. 609.
36 *Jimmy Carter Presidential Library*, Atlanta, Georgia (hereafter *JCL*), Staff Offices, Domestic Policy Staff, Eizenstat box 148, folder: Aviation Airline Regulatory Reform, Message to Congress 4 March 1977, attached to Eizenstat to Carter, 22 February 1977.
37 *JCL*, JCL WHCF, subject file, box CA-1, folder: 9/1/78–12/31/78, 'US Policy for the Conduct of International Air Transportation Negotiations', 21 August 1978.
38 'International Air Transportation Competition Act of 1979', US PL 96–192, 15 February 1980.
39 CAB order 78–6–78, 12 June 1978.
40 ECAC was established through the good offices of the Council of Europe and ICAO in 1955. It reflects the work of and cooperates closely with ICAO.
41 The US pulled back from dramatic removal of antitrust immunity, but the issue refused to go away, as was demonstrated in the previous section. Jönsson argues that IATA heavily orchestrated opposition to the SCO, but this is somewhat misleading. It publicized and disseminated information and helped coordinate opposition, but at the time few outside the USA favoured price liberalization. IATA was on the winning side from the very start. Also Jönsson's claim that the US attempt at regime change failed now looks premature. In the longer term US actions did result in what Jönsson would term regime change. Successfully pushing the US to withdraw the SCO was a Pyrrhic victory. See Jönsson, *International Aviation*, chapter 7 and Dobson, *Flying in the Face*

of Competition; and Alan P. Dobson and Joe Mckinney, 'Sovereignty, Politics and US International Airline Policy', *Journal of Air Law and Commerce*, 74(iii), (2009), pp. 527–53.

42 Author interview with Cyril Murphy, Vice President for International Affairs, United Airlines, 1 July 1991.

43 R. Pryke, *Competition among International Airlines*, Aldershot: Gower, 1987, pp. 52–3.

44 B.S. Peterson, *Bluestreak: Inside Jetblue, the Upstart that Rocked the Industry*, New York: Portfolio, 2004, p. 101.

45 For the story of changes in Europe see Alan P. Dobson, *Globalization and Regional Integration: The Origins, Development and Impact of the Single European Aviation Market*, London, Routledge, 2007.

46 John R. Steele speech ECAC-EU Dialogue, 29 April 2005, www.prismaconsulting.com/EC, retrieved 7 December 2005.

47 Author interview Murphy.

48 Renouncing the ASA was provided for in the agreement, as was a 12-month re-negotiation period.

49 Alan P. Dobson, 'Regulation or Competition: Negotiating the Anglo-American Air Services Agreement of 1977', *The Journal of Transport History*, 15, (1994), pp. 144–65.

50 Author interview with Edmund Dell, Secretary of State for Trade 1976–78, London, 8 December 1989.

51 "Bermuda 2" – Air Services Agreement Between the Government of the United States of America and the Government of Great Britain and Northern Ireland including amendments through 1980, Annex 7, *London Airports*, p. 69. Copy courtesy of US Department of Transportation. See also Alan P. Dobson, 'Not the Third World War: The US-UK Heathrow Succession Rights Affair and Anglo-American Relations', *Diplomacy and Statecraft* 25(iii), (2014), pp. 529–49.

52 Author interview with Murphy.

53 Author interview with Jeffrey N. Shane, Assistant Secretary for Policy and International Affairs, US Department of Transportation, 5 April 1991.

54 US Department of Transportation unpublished study, December 1992, cited in Jeffrey N. Shane, 'Under Secretary for Policy, U.S. Department of Transportation, 'Air Transport Liberalization: Ideal and Ordeal', Royal Aeronautical Society, Montreal, 8 December 2005.

Annex 1

Resolution adopted at the extraordinary session of the council on 8 December 2014 on the occasion of the seventieth anniversary of the signing of the Chicago Convention

Whereas 7 December 2014 marks the Seventieth Anniversary of the signing in Chicago of the *Convention on International Civil Aviation*, also known as the Chicago Convention;

Convinced that the fundamental aims and objectives of the Chicago Convention remain as relevant today as when they were conceived in 1944;

Recognizing that the safe and orderly growth of civil aviation that has been achieved over the past seventy years has delivered many positive socioeconomic benefits to humanity;

Determined to ensure that international civil aviation will continue to contribute to the promotion of global peace and security, social integration among the peoples of the world, economic prosperity of nations, and sustainable development for future generations; and

Considering that there remains a strong and ongoing need for the international community to continue forging consensus-based progress in international civil aviation and to build on the foundations that were laid in Chicago seventy years ago;

The Council of the International Civil Aviation Organization (ICAO), on the occasion of this 70th Anniversary of the signing of the Chicago Convention:

1 *Pays tribute* to the leadership, vision and cooperative spirit of the signatories of the Chicago Convention, who came together seventy years ago to create and preserve friendship and understanding among the nations and peoples of the world in the development of international civil aviation;

2 *Emphasizes* the essential role that ICAO plays as a global forum for cooperation among its Member States and the civil aviation community, and as a standard-setting body for the safe and orderly development of international civil aviation;

3 *Reiterates* the need for ICAO, as a specialized agency in relationship with the United Nations, to continue to take a leadership role in the development of principles, standards, agreements and arrangements for global civil aviation, thereby contributing to peace and prosperity in the world;

4   *Encourages* all Member States of ICAO to continue to promote the ideals and principles of the *Convention on International Civil Aviation* and compliance with its provisions;

5   *Acknowledges* the critical need for continued ICAO efforts aimed at identifying the challenges posed by increases in global air transport demand and capacity, as well as the opportunities offered by new and emerging technologies, and to address those challenges and take advantage of those opportunities in order to achieve the safe, secure and sustainable growth of the international civil aviation system; and

6   *Invites* all stakeholders, including Member States and relevant organizations of the global civil aviation community, to continue sharing and promoting best practices and working together through ICAO in support of a worldwide air transport system, which serves and benefits all nations and peoples of the world.

5 Creating the single European aviation market

Just as it's not supposed to be possible for a bumblebee to fly, it shouldn't have been politically possible to deregulate the airline industry.[1]

The Commission suggests that American-style deregulation would not work in the present European Context.[2]

Introduction: the focus and the challenge

The SEAM is the greatest achievement to date in cutting the Gordian knot between national air sovereignty and international airline operations. Others have followed suit, or are in the process of doing something similar, but the SEAM stands out as the beacon of what can be achieved in terms of removing the traditional barriers that have fragmented the industry.[3] Originally 12 states began the process and now 28 nation states enjoy the release from market dysfunction caused by national boundaries. Much can be learnt for the wider aviation industry from the creation of the SEAM, but the learning will not be easy.[4] The EU is a novel creation of contemporary times, which defies easy characterization and poses difficult challenges for explanation. It exposes inadequacies in the language and concepts of IR; for example the concepts of union and nation state seem logically incompatible and yet they exist cheek by jowl in Europe. Politicians and scholars argue endlessly over the EU's gestation, development and current state: from the functional and neo-functionalist explanations of scholars such as Ernst B. Haas to the federalism of Altiero Spinelli to the kind of plague on all theoretical houses of the eminent economic historian Alan Milward. The latter argued that the European Community was the savior of the nation state in Europe, not its nemesis, and that the states came together as a result of individual government decisions in the historical context provided by war and cold war. For him the European Community was not so much a federation as an inter-governmental confederacy driven by state needs to deliver more effectively prosperity, social welfare and security. A somewhat ahistorical version of this abides currently in the work of the inter-governmentalist Andrew Moravscik.[5] All these approaches provide important perspectives and insights into the workings of the EU and the creation of a level playing field for the civil aviation industry. If the global international civil aviation market aspires to be something similar then there may be much to learn from the European experience. But, of course, the European experience cannot be isolated from developments elsewhere. Much of the original impetus for change in Europe came from the US.

Deregulation was the key new dynamic, although Europeans tended to see it as an American phenomenon and the term was not often used to describe what went on in the European Community (EC)/EU[6] between 1987 and 1997 when the SEAM was crafted. Liberalization was more commonly used, but both terms raise an essential question: What was it all supposed to produce? Again, at the time, there were differences of opinion on each side of the Atlantic and within the US and the EC/EU; however, it is possible to identify a cluster of shared objectives that established roadmaps that both followed towards more liberal objectives. In 2007 their respective ambitions allowed them to make an historic deal on an EU-US ASA, but that also camouflaged the fact that they also ideally favored two different paths as the ultimate way forward for international aviation.

Firstly, the US and the EC/EU wanted a more liberal, lighter regulated and more competitive airline industry, though it took the latter some time to settle on that because of the reluctance of what was initially an overwhelming majority of the Member States which favored more or less the *status quo*. Some differences between the US and the EU abided, but gradually there was a definite convergence in the way the industry operated on either side of the Atlantic. Secondly, there was a renewed common commitment to improve harmonization of standards and safety provisions, most significantly of all in the field of security. Thirdly, and perhaps most importantly of all, there emerged a new vision for international civil aviation in the US cast in terms of open-skies. The Europeans eventually bought into that vision, but then to the surprise of many moved beyond it to the concept of an open transatlantic aviation area. These will be major themes of the next chapter, but first it is important to examine Europe's radical and vital contributions: not just in theory, but also in the practical building of the SEAM.

In the 1970s the suggestion that Europe might trail-blaze for international civil aviation would have been met with derision and disbelief. Europe reacted with intense hostility to the idea of deregulation and such attitudes were partly symptomatic of long-standing differences between European social democracy and US liberal, capitalist democracy. At a time of worldwide economic recession, overcapacity in the airline industry and accumulation of huge losses, the US turned to deregulation, liberalization and acceptance of more market forces. In contrast, in Europe, regulation was embraced even more tightly and state airlines were bailed out with more subsidies and government help. These observations also apply to Britain, well exemplified in its negotiation of Bermuda 2, even though it is often conceived of as standing somewhere in between Europe and the US on social and economic matters.

In 1978 the European scheduled airline market was moving in the opposite direction to its US counterpart. It was a non-competitive, commercially inefficient, cartel-type operation with dominant players, which was not responsive to public needs and was organized around the nation state and not the European Community.[7] Furthermore, of the 12 Member States at the time, only Britain and the Netherlands were interested in change, which meant that there were going to be massive problems in trying to introduce new policies through the Council of Ministers, the highest political decision-taking and executive organ of the EC. The other 10 Member States, the overwhelming majority of scheduled carriers and their main professional organization, the Association of European Airlines (AEA), unanimously opposed reform. There was virtually no public pressure for change, as most members of the travelling public, when they flew at all, were carried by the more competitive and cheaper charter airline industry.[8] And the Commission, the Community's executive bureaucracy and guardian of the founding Rome Treaty, could provide little leadership with only a tiny group of officials, largely inexperienced, devoted to air transport in the European Commission's Directorate General VII for Transport (DG VII). Nevertheless, by 1997 the situation had been radically transformed with the creation of the SEAM.

The questions to be addressed in this chapter are: What brought about this astonishing and seemingly most unlikely metamorphosis in Europe? How did a small majority of the Member States and the Commission manage to liberalize the European aviation market in three stages between 1987 and 1997? How did they overcome strongly embedded vested interests that stood against change? What were the dynamics that came together to push change along? And what might we learn from it regarding more ambitious aspirations for a truly globalized industry? The last question is very apt because while the questions above apply here to the European market, they might also be posed generically to interrogate what might be done in the global market.

The size of the problem and the thinking in Europe

The beginnings of the EC looked auspicious for airline competition. The Treaty of Rome laid the foundation for a common market and an ever-closer union of states characterized by competition and economic and social cohesion.[9] The Treaty provided for a competitive market (Article 3), underpinned by competition rules prohibiting both cartel arrangements and market abuse by dominant actors (Articles 85–91). There were to be free movement of workers and a right of establishment for companies anywhere in the Community (Articles 52–58). And an integral part of all this was a common transport policy (CTP: Title 4, Articles 74–84), something essential for opening up the state-centric transport systems of Europe.[10] In particular, one would have thought that this would have empowered airlines; however, for many years, it did not. The airline industry was left bereft of competition because of inaction, procrastination and above all vested interests and protectionist nationalism.

Integrating national transport systems was difficult and this was recognized in Title 4, which specifically acknowledged that there would be a two-track, two-speed approach: for rail, road and inland waterways the provisions of Title 4 applied immediately; but it was left to the discretion of the Council of Ministers to decide how to proceed on sea and air transport.[11] 'The Council may, acting by a qualified majority, decide whether, to what extent and by what procedure appropriate provisions may be laid down for sea and air transport.'[12] In Febru-ary 1962, the Council of Ministers adopted Regulation 17 implementing the competition provisions of the Treaty of Rome and for a short time this looked promising for air transport, but the Council dashed such hopes in November 1962 when it adopted Regulation 141, which retrospectively withdrew both sea and air transport from the scope of Regulation 17: 'it was felt that . . . some kind of Com-munity policy should be developed before competition rules could be applied.'[13]

The Council, in fact, took no effective steps whatsoever to develop such policy, but a dozen years later in 1974 the European Court of Justice gave notice that the airline industry should not be so completely sundered from the competition rules. In the French Seamen's Case, the issue before the Court was whether or not a quota reserving jobs for French nationals contravened provisions of the Treaty. The Court found it did on the grounds that air and sea transport 'remains, on the same basis as the other modes of transport, subject to the general rules of the Treaty. It thus follows that the application of Articles 48 to 51 to the sphere of sea transport is not optional but obligatory for Member States.'[14] Such quotas in other words were discriminatory and anticompetitive. Unfortunately, this did not entirely disperse the ambiguity surrounding air transport and the competition rules, but it did edge a little further towards the idea that they might be applicable. This gave some encouragement to those in the Commission who wanted reform, but it was several years before any line of advance could be developed because there was no real power base or consumer demand calling for change.

The creation of the SEAM might best be understood as developing in stages through the interplay of several dynamics. The first is the impact of new ideas closely linked with market forces. This has already been considered in Chapter 4 and so only requires a brief mention here in order to provide a more detailed Euro-pean context. The other two dynamics require full sections of their own.

One of the problems in Europe and, though to a lesser extent, in the US was the post-war dominance of conventional economic wisdom derived largely from Keynesianism and the perceived nature of the airline industry: that regulation and price controls were essential. However as the previous chapter demonstrated, eco-nomic difficulties and Keynesianism's seeming inability to respond effectively to the economic challenges that emerged in the 1970s, and particularly to remedy the ills of stagflation, resulted in the evolution and eventual adoption of new economic thinking. This paradigm shift was an important prerequisite for deregulation/liberalization of the airline industry. Gradually, during the late 1970s and the 1980s, the dynamic interplay between ideas and market forces unleashed in the US spread abroad, encouraging home-grown desires for reform. In Britain, such ideas took hold when Margaret Thatcher came to power in 1979 and both in Brit-ain and the Netherlands a more favorable environment for change in the airline industry arose. There were now at least powerful voices calling for reform from two out of the 12 Member States.

More surprising was a development in ECAC. ECAC was notoriously conserva-tive in outlook, but, in the early 1980s, liberal British and Dutch officials hijacked one of its policy studies to produce the COMPAS Report.[15] This proved important in several ways, including empowering the voices of reform within DG VII. With one eye on US experience, the COMPAS Report argued that competition in civil aviation depended upon three inextricably linked factors: route entry; capacity; and fares. Action in one without action elsewhere would be ineffective. For competition to flourish all three areas would need adjustment. Those within the EC Commission, who later drafted the reform proposals for the SEAM, thought this helped set a new intellectual framework for airline reform.[16] Frederick Sorensen, a soft-spoken Dane and the key player in aviation throughout the 1980s and 1990s and beyond in the Commission's DG VII, thought that 'it had a tremendous influence.' In particular, ideas in the COMPAS Report helped in the process of modifying and developing the Commission's proposals for reform. Also it had important tactical impact. It helped to mold the thinking of officials from the Member States of the EC in middle management echelons and, as time passed and momentum for reform grew, those officials helped to mediate proposals for reform between the Commission and the political leadership in their respective nation states.[17] In short it helped educate officials about what was needed and what was possible and facilitated a paradigm shift in official thinking. And that thinking had something to ponder on by the mid-1980s: Europeans were paying over twice as much to fly 1,000 miles in Europe than they would to fly 5,000 miles on a US carrier from Europe to San Francisco.[18] These changes helped create an intellectual environment in which legal, political and bureaucratic actions could be taken and be more effective in driving reform forward.

The second important dynamic involved initiatives and strategies from the European Court of Justice and the Commission. Such dynamics are given primary emphasis by various schools of functionalism and liberal institutionalism, all of which generally fall under the broader category of Idealism. The third dynamic is provided by the drive for reform from Britain and the Netherlands and their close cooperation (for most of the time) with the Commission. Inter-governmentalism and other theoretical approaches aligned with Realism emphasize this approach.[19] The two dynamics of the Court and the Commission and the initiatives taken by Britain and the Netherlands working with the Commission will be the subject of the next two sections and, along with the changes in economic and political thinking, were the crucial elements in change. In contrast, consumer lobby groups and industry organizations played roles of only minor significance. Of their ranks, the AEA and labor unions were probably the most influential and their shared position was resolutely that of regulatory conservatism.[20]

The court and the commission

Between 1974 and 1984 little altered in the European scheduled airline system, but the threat from market forces released by the US hung over all and the agents of change and their ideas were gaining strength. In January 1977, Roy Jenkins of Britain took the Presidency of the Commission, and among other things called for the establishment of a special working party on air transport.[21] The Council's Committee of Permanent Representatives (COREPER) duly complied and a Working Party on Transport Questions was charged with looking specifically at civil aviation matters. More importantly, these developments also prompted the creation of a specialist air transport policy unit in DG VII, which recruited Sorensen, whose views became central to later developments. This is how he expressed them in the spring of 1991:

> Air transport policy must on the one hand ensure a financially healthy indus-
> try providing a certain economic stability and reasonable conditions for
> employment and on the other hand ensure a market structure where air carri-
> ers can adapt their operations according to the growth and shifts in the market
> and provide sufficient choice of services to the consumer at reasonable prices.
> Experience has shown that a certain modicum of competition is desirable in
> order to avoid a stale cost-plus system. However, a competitive market may
> lead to abuse or uncompetitive behaviour and we aim to avoid that through
> benign regulatory rules.[22]

This was not US-style deregulation, but it was something far closer to it than the existing European aviation system. In pursuit of this vision, DG VII collaborated with DG IV, the Competition Directorate General, the British and the Dutch. By 1985 DG VII had achieved four modest results, Memorandum 1 and 2 on aviation reform policy, an agreement for powers of consultation between the Commission and the Member States, and a Regional Services Directive.[23] The two memoranda did not result in new policies immediately, but they did stimulate debate and set out how gradual reform of route entry, capacity and fares would produce a more competitive industry and one that would benefit consumers. On regional services, many months passed before a watered-down version of the Commission's original proposal emerged as a directive in July 1983. And while DG VII was generally disappointed, Sorensen felt that they still 'got a result [because] it acts on mar-ket access, capacity, and fares . . . it is important that all those three areas were addressed.'[24] These principles, laid out in the COMPAS Report, had been dis-cussed at length and agreed between the Commission and British officials who, like Sorensen, expected them to 'set a pattern for action in other sectors.'[25] The fourth achievement – on consultation powers – looked dry and bureaucratic, but it provided important powers for the Commission. In May 1985 they were invoked for the first time to investigate whether price coordination by European airlines might be contrary to the competition rules.

These developments were notable and even more so when placed in the context of broader developments promising action on the Single Market. The Cockfield White Paper, named after Lord Arthur Cockfield, the Commissioner for the Inter-nal Market, identified 279 specific actions that were needed to complete the Single Market by the target date of 1992.[26] Furthermore, there was a specific warning

> that if no action was taken [by the Council] concerning the application of the
> competition rules to air transport, [the Commission] would have to take note
> of infringements and authorize Member States to take measures determined
> by it in accordance with Article 89.[27]

This amounted to a much more supportive context for developing the SEAM, with its threat of legal drivers and time limits. There was also a new sense of purpose in the Commission under the powerful leadership of Jacques Delors and, in DG IV, Commissioner Peter Sutherland from Eire was strongly committed to applying the competition rules in the airline sector. At the EC Milan Summit, 28–29 June 1985, the Cockfield White Paper was accepted. The Member States were now committed to the achievement of a Single Market by the end of 1992 and air transport was specifically included in that objective. Matters seemed about to move forward.

However, things were not moving swiftly in the Council. This occasioned growing criticisms, which emboldened the Commission to declare itself 'profoundly disappointed with the lack of progress' on Memorandum 2, urged the Council to give the civil aviation dossier greater priority and robustly announced:

> The Commission is in no way prepared to sacrifice its objective of creating more competition in the air transport sector. To do so would be to fail in our obligations under the Treaty and to fail our duty to the European citizen. If the negotiating process does not work, we shall have no option but to use other weapons.[28]

These 'other weapons' were legal in form. Sutherland had made it clear that DG IV would use the competition rules to bring cases before the European Court of Justice if satisfactory reforms were not forthcoming. At the end of April 1985 Director General of Transport John Steele explained matters to Transport Commissioner Stanley Clinton Davis. The airlines, subject to certain conditions being met, would be exempted from the application of the competition articles, but in return the Member States would have to accept Council provisions that would 'allow up to a point commercial competition to operate.'[29] The alternative would be to take action in the European Court of Justice. In theory this sounded fine, but the legal position on the application of the competition rules was still uncertain. It was not until a year later in the *Nouvelles Frontières* case that it became clear.

The Court overturned the previous exemption of the airline industry from the competition rules of the Rome Treaty and now declared that they should be applied.[30] Ambiguity any longer, there was not. The Commission's Legal Service noted:

> The main point at which the judgement breaks new ground is its finding that the competition rules do apply to air transport.
>
> Under Article 89, the Court said the Commission may, on application by a Member State or on its own initiative, investigate "cases of suspected infringement" of Articles 85 and 86, and if it finds that there has been infringement it may propose "appropriate measures to bring it to an end."[31]

This honed the Commission's legal weapon. It now had a clear mandate: it could apply the competition rules as required by EC law and throw the existing system into convulsions. Alternatively, it could urge the Member States to take action through the Council to make provision for a SEAM and offer the inducement of temporary block exemptions from the competition rules in return for gradual movement into a more liberal regime.

The Transport Council now came under considerable pressures, including statements from the heads-of-government European Council Meeting at The Hague held between 26 and 27 June. The call was for speedy action in the light of the *Nouvelles Frontières* case on tariffs, capacity and market access. Thus, although the Transport Council made no decisions of real substance it did issue, as Sorensen had suspected it would, a statement of principles, which proved to be a lot more significant than has generally been acknowledged. It confirmed:

i   the need for . . . increased competition in intra-Community air services as regards tariffs, capacity and market entry, in conformity with the competition rules of the Treaty;

ii   such a system should be established gradually. To that end, the Council agrees on an initial period of application of three years, during which the Council will review developments and take decisions on further steps in order to achieve the objective of the completion of the internal market by the year 1992.[32]

The Council had set a three-year period for a first phase and established clearly that further reform would follow in order to complete the SEAM by the end of 1992. There was a real commitment here driven by the legal mandate of having to apply the competition rules throughout the transport sector and reinforced by the broader political commitment made by the Community to realize the Single Market by 1992.

The Commission now decided to brandish its main weapon. DG IV drafted letters for Sutherland to dispatch on 18 July to 10 major EC airlines. The letters explained that the Commission was acting in accordance with the conclusions of the European Council at The Hague and under its obligations made clear by the *Nouvelles Frontières* case to apply the competition rules of the Treaty under the auspices of Article 89(1). The letter to BA, one of the targeted airlines, continued:

In proceeding under Article 89, the Commission wishes to open a formal dialogue with your company with a view to ensuring that your agreements and practices are brought into conformity with the competition rules of the Treaty as soon as possible. . . . The Commission considers having examined the information currently available to it, that there are good grounds for finding that British Airways has infringed the provisions of Article 85 of the EEC Treaty.[33]

All that remained was to see how effective the inducement of granting exemptions from the competition rules in return for movement towards reform would be.

The inter-governmental perspective

Pressures for reform empowered what was initially a small minority of the Member States to push through three packages of reform. In doing this, they gradually drew in the support of others, which began to appreciate the possible benefits of liberalization. Some states recognized specific benefits for their own airlines: for example, Eire decided to support the first package of reform because it delivered Fifth Freedom rights from the UK. Others felt coerced by legal realities. And finally, a sense of the inevitability of it all developed, something which eventually even infected France, the staunchest of the regulatory conservative states. Space does not allow a full account of these developments, but a sense of them can be conveyed by briefly looking at Packages 1 and 3 and by examining the passage of Package 2 in more detail.

Package 1 took the form of two directives, one on airfares and capacity and market access, and two enabling regulations on the application of the competition rules and on agreements and cartel practices.[34] On fares, approval by both states on a route – 'double approval' – was required, but that was modified by the caveat that fares must be approved if they were reasonably related to long-term, fully allocated costs and speedy arbitration procedures would resolve disputes. There was also a zone of flexibility within which fares were to be automatically approved: in the discount zone between 90% and 65% of normal economy fare and in the deep discount zone between 65% and 45% of the normal economy fare. One analyst observed: 'Where liberal arrangements already exist, the new latitude will have little effect . . . but it will oblige hitherto less liberal states to approve a wider range of promotional fares.'[35]

Capacity and market access were dealt with together in the same directive. The British had fought hard and long (though not as hard as the Dutch would have liked) for reform of capacity agreements. The final compromise permitted 45%/55% splits between airlines moving to 40%/60% in the third year. There was acceptance of multiple designation, Fifth Freedom rights and the extension of Third and Fourth Freedom rights on regional routes to include major airports. This was progress, but there were many qualifying conditions that restricted market impact. The enabling regulations allowed the application of the competition rules and made provision for block exemptions in three areas: firstly, capacity sharing, revenue sharing, fare consultations, scheduling and take-off and landing slot allocations; secondly, the use of computer reservation systems; and thirdly, ground handling and in-flight catering services. These exemptions would not, however, last forever. The Commission now had broad powers of investigation and the authority to impose substantial fines on airlines if they departed from this more liberal regime. Furthermore, it was made plain that Package 1 was only temporary. The Council would revise it no later than 30 June 1990 into a second package, and that would lead on to a fully fledged SEAM by the end of 1992 as part of the wider agenda involved in creating the Single Market.[36]

Momentum continued and at the end of July 1989 *The Independent* newspaper announced:

> Sir Leon Brittan, European Community commissioner for competition policy, has just unveiled proposals, which if accepted by EC transport ministers, would dismantle the maze of restrictions currently preventing competition in the air.[37]

That was not to happen immediately, but there was substantial delivery with Package 2 and a promise of significantly more to come.

Proposals were largely crafted through an interplay between British and Commission officials from DG IV and DG VII. The result was radical. Package 2 proposed double disapproval pricing and the application of the competition rules to fares on routes to third parties outside the Community. It wanted to phase out capacity restrictions, impose a liberal licensing regime, open cabotage, lift restrictions on Fifth Freedoms, lower thresholds for multiple designation and open more airports to regional traffic.

Karel van Miert, the new Transport Commissioner, and Brittan resolutely pushed the full range of proposals through to acceptance by the Commission in a series of meetings in July 1989.[38] Both French Commissioners Christiane Scrivener and Jacques Delors, however, notably voted against their acceptance and France led the subsequent counterattack on the more liberal aspects of Package 2.

As soon as the Commission's proposals were published, the French convened an informal meeting of the Transport Council 'rushing to set a corset of Council decisions around the Commission's proposals in order to restrict the action and policies' that its successor presidency, that of the Irish, would be able to pursue in the final months before the deadline for Package 2 in June 1990.[39] Supported by the AEA and trade union representations, the French urged caution and the need for harmonization, adequate social provisions, maintaining exemptions from the competition rules and the continuation of bilateral relations rather than a move to multilateral competence for the Commission. The French presidency set up a High-Level Group (HLG) composed of Directors' General of Civil Aviation to hammer out detailed policies. However, President Mitterand, sensitive to the need for France to make a success of its presidency and with a broader political agenda than those dealing with aviation, issued instructions to French officials in October that they should be prepared to make concessions in order to make the French overall presidency, including in the Transport Council, a success. A senior British official, Handley Stevens, discerned some impact from that in meetings of the HLG on 15–16 November, which tabled a draft set of decisions agreed by majority vote. On the other hand, ex-government official and long-time aviation analyst John Loder noted of the same outcome: 'In two major respects it overturns the Commission's proposals: it rejects Double Disapproval of air fares and substitutes a new [discount] zone', which was remarkably similar to one advocated by conservative forces in the European Parliament, the AEA and ECAC.

And furthermore, 'it rejects moves to a 75/25% country pair capacity balance.'[40] When these decisions were referred to the COREPER a few days later they were approved. Furthermore the market access provisions seemed to 'reject the Commission's proposals on right of establishment and removal of States' rights to maintain national airline monopolies . . . Similarly cabotage [was] to remain subject of "deep study".'[41]

It was in the final Council session 4–5 December and in two further meetings of the HLG that the situation was retrieved, at least insofar as establishing a future timetable for implementing what the Commission had wanted to achieve immediately through Package 2. It was at this point that the French really shifted their position. If they had wanted to they could have led the regulatory conservative majority and outvoted the reform states led by Britain and the Netherlands. Even under new rules for qualified majority voting the liberalizers could not muster enough votes to push things through.

In substance Package 2 did not move liberalization much further forward.[42] The Council postponed action on operating and route licensing and generally on the introduction of double disapproval pricing, all of which if introduced would have strengthened 'opportunities for new carriers to enter the market and compete effectively.'[43] Other proposals from the Commission on entry into the marketplace had been diluted, capacity restrictions continued for the time being and the idea of extending the competition rules to pricing on routes to third parties outside the Community had been set aside. All this was bad news for the reformers, but the good news was that most of these issues had only been postponed: the forces of regulatory conservatism had not buried them. In the meetings of the HLG on 4–5 December various timetables were accepted. There would have to be uniform licensing criteria by July 1992. Double disapproval pricing and capacity freedom would be introduced by January 1993. And, though hedged with more uncertainty about delivery, cabotage would have to be opened.

One British official who observed the deterioration of the French position commented:

> The French were like fish out of water. They thought that they could control this process. It was fascinating to watch them lose it. . . . They were getting desperate about the whole thing. They tried to link it to harmonization and other things. None of them worked. You know, it was just fascinating.[44]

The French made tactical errors of judgement and were coerced into further change by the market and policy-preference dynamics already at play in the industry. More specifically there appear to be four reasons why they moved to accept gradual liberalization: the need to be seen as good Europeans and achieve something during their presidency; the need to accept the reality of the legal situation; the opportunity to benefit Air France; and resignation to the fact that reform was now inevitable.

Mitterand's position and instructions to officials were clearly important and a senior official in DG VII, looking back, thought that the French changed their stance because of 'political consideration [about] Europe. I think that was the main thing, at least, that was my impression.'[45] In other words opposition to air transport reform was becoming tantamount to opposition to the European idea itself. In addition the French Transport Minister Michel Delebarre had personal political ambitions, which would be furthered by a success story from the Transport Council.[46]

The second thing confronting the French was that: 'Legally speaking there was no possibility for [them] to resist . . . they would have to accommodate us [i.e. the Commission].'[47] Nicholas Argyris, Head of the Division for Transport and Tourist Industries in DG IV, explained the hold that the Commission had over those Member States reluctant to accept liberalization: 'The Commission's willingness to renew the block exemptions up to the end of 1992, depends on the Council adopting proposals of the kind which have been tabled.'[48]

The third and fourth factors to affect the French position were a combination of the realization that liberalization was going to happen whatever they might do and that reform could offer advantages for Air France. Less than a year after the French presidency agreed to what became the substance of Package 2 and its timetabled promises for further liberalization, Air France received a decision from the Commission that would strengthen its position in a more liberal dispensation. The main problem that eventually struck down both TWA and Pan Am in the US was their lack of adequate domestic feeder systems for their long-haul operations. That, Air France determined, was not going to happen to it. In November 1990 the 'Commission . . . cleared Air France's takeover of French carriers Air Inter and *Union de Transport Aérien* (UTA) giving the state-owned flag carrier its own domestic service network and access to all French international routes.'[49] In return Air France had had to agree to open up eight domestic and 50 international routes to domestic French and overseas airlines. Leon Brittan commented that the French had opened up their market in 'a way that would have been unthinkable a few months ago.'[50] That might have been true, but what was happening here was not so much an opening up of the French market as a re-positioning, through collusion between Air France and the French government to sustain the national flag carrier's dominant position and reap what rewards it might from liberalization. Lord King, Chairman of BA, certainly saw things in that light when he spoke at the Royal Aeronautical Society in May 1991:

> It is instructive to note how France is preparing for these [competitive] challenges. Air France, Air Inter and UTA have been consolidated in a single airline, which now carries many more passengers than British Airways. The number of European destinations served by Air France has been rapidly increased. The authorities are investing heavily in Charles De Gaulle and in the surface transport systems, which serve that airport. The aim is to displace Heathrow as Europe's premier gateway and make Paris Western Europe's premier hub.[51]

In a way, once liberalization of the marketplace began it became contagious. The forces of globalization were stripping the wings off the conservative regulatory project's flying machine. If European airlines wanted to continue to operate they would have to become more competitive. That did not mean deregulation. In Europe it meant getting rid of the old cartel-style system of airline-government collusion and adopting new measures of regulation that would encourage competition to thrive. When one adds all these factors together – bad judgement, the need to be seen as good Europeans and have achievements credited to the French presidency, legal realities, and the effects of and opportunities offered by what seemed an inevitable opening up of the European airline system – it becomes evident why the French position changed. And with it, the final door opened to the SEAM.

Bringing it all together

> It's a process [liberalization]. First of all we need to put in place all the rules, which are necessary for this to occur. Airlines have to adapt themselves to a new situation and make use of opportunities and then we have to see actual evidence of competition between airlines.[52]

Package 3 was now mandatory and, in Council on 22 June 1992, attempts by France, Germany and Italy to put the brakes on liberalization by linking forward movement to progress on external relations and take-off and landing slot allocation rules, both of which were heavily bogged down, failed.[53] On market access there were disappointments for the liberalizers with the timetable, but that was all that it amounted to. Full introduction of cabotage rights was delayed on the insistence of France, Germany, Greece and Italy until 1997. Market access was eased with unrestricted Fifths made available between most Community airports and with the introduction of Seventh Freedom rights, which allowed the airline of one country to originate a flight in another and fly to a third party. Access could be denied on environmental or congestion grounds, but such denials had to be non-discriminatory and were subject to Commission adjudication. National ownership was abolished as of January 1993 and replaced by the concept of Community carriers: this became the driver, which eventually delivered significant power over external relations into the hands of the Commission. The most radical aspect of Package 3 was on licensing: Member States had 'to grant a licence to any airline which meets the (not exacting) standards.'[54] Such licensing combined with other liberal market access policies and a liberal fares regime amounted to a formidable step forward in encouraging a multi-airline competitive regime. By 1997, with the exception of external relations where Member States' bilateral ASAs delivered differentiated commercial advantages, there was now a level commercial playing field with an effective SEAM, providing that the airlines would actually exploit the situation. The vision of the COMPAS Report had come to pass: liberal route access, liberal capacity and liberal pricing.

Early reports were sanguine about intent and Commission action, but thin on the substance of market change. European carriers continued to lag behind US productivity levels by 20%, Fifth Freedoms and what had previously been national cabotage rights were not largely used and there was little increase in multiple designations.[55] In 1995 a UK Civil Aviation Authority (CAA) report was upbeat, at least about the decisiveness of the Commission in implementing Package 3: 'overall, liberalisation has been implemented with impressive success.'[56] However, *The Financial Times* pointed out that the CAA's optimism was hard to justify 'by results in the market.'[57] It was correct. There had been some improvements among previously heavily restricted markets such as Germany's and Spain's, the independent airline British Midland (BM) had sparked some price competition and there was a small decline in the dominance of the national carriers, but: 'Most damningly, Europe's notoriously high air fares have been slow to fall.'[58]

There had always been the worry among Commission officials that no matter how the system might be changed, if the airlines refused to compete, it would all be to no avail. There had been some encouraging developments in the 1980s with existing airlines becoming more competitive, such as the privately owned BM, as well as KLM and BA, which, after much delay because of legal and political obstacles, had been successfully privatized by sale to shareholders in 1987,[59] but these developments were not seen to be sufficient for overall success by the reformers. And indeed, the first three years had not been very auspicious, but things were about to change. Firstly, the industry was finally emerging from the recession precipitated by the First Gulf War and, secondly, it was on the cusp of dramatic innovation that was to be injected into the system by no-frills, low-cost airlines. A month after the CAA report on the SEAM, Stelios Haji-Ioannou's EasyJet took its first booking. EasyJet along with Ryanair became the no-frills market leaders. In addition to spawning a host of imitators such as Debonair, they also prompted BA, KLM, BM and Virgin to launch, respectively, Go, Buzz, BMI Baby and Virgin Express and airlines such as Braathens and Maersk Air to develop copycat strategies. By 1998 Ryanair was offering a £99 return fare between London and Stockholm, which compared favorably with BA's £500 fare. Not surprisingly reports on the success of the SEAM after 1995 became increasingly fulsome in praise of the results of Package 3 and of the way liberalization was delivering results to industry and consumers alike.

By 1996 routes had increased from 490 in 1993 to 520. Those using promotional fares rose from 60.5% to 70.9% of total passengers over the decade from 1985. Over 30% of routes were now served by two operators and 6% by three or more and 90–95% of passengers were travelling at significantly lower prices than in 1993. The Commission recognized that more still needed to be done. The price of fully flexible fares, favored by business people, continued to rise significantly and there was lack of transparency about how they were set. Infrastructure costs were high at 25% of total airline operating costs and were 40% higher than in the US. Even so, the general feeling was that the internal market was 'flourishing'.[60] One major problem remained, however: external relations and the differentiated advantages that the Member States drew from their bilateral ASAs with non-Member States. But this will have to await the next chapter, as it became a key issue in the development of the vision for a transatlantic common aviation area and that in turn was seen by some as a model that would draw in the rest of the world, thus morphing a regional aviation market into a truly global one.

Conclusion

All explanations of highly complex market and political change oversimplify. For exegetical and pedagogic reasons, the process of integration has been set out largely as the result of three important dynamics: the force of ideas and the marketplace; the strategies and actions of the Court and the Commission; and the drive initially by Britain and the Netherlands to extract liberal reform decisions from the Council of Ministers. However, it should be clear that at all times these three forces interplayed with each other as well as being forces in their own right. And the only way to demonstrate that effectively has been to indulge in more historical detail than has usually been the case in this study. In addition to the three key dynamics identified, there was a role for public opinion and for pressure groups, but for much of the process of reform, public opinion was muted or else the voices of regulatory conservatism spoke more loudly. Having said this to qualify in general terms what has been set out here as the explanation of the creation of the SEAM, it should also be reaffirmed that the process generally followed the direction of early momentum created by ideas and market forces. In the more favorable context that this created, the Court and the Commission worked hard to bring about incremental change, develop expertise and form alliances with those Member States that favored reform. These strategies facilitated the exploitation of Court decisions to create powerful legal drivers at a time when there was a broad renewal of the momentum for consummating the European Single Market. Then, and really only then, was it possible for high-level political action to grasp the initiative. With ongoing help from the Commission, the Court, and impact from market forces, it was possible to implement the three packages of reform.

What those three packages of reform achieved was quite unique and – in historical context – astounding. The SEAM went beyond the most liberal proposal that was in real contention at the Chicago Conference, namely a multilateral agreement for a commercial regime based on the automatic exchange of the Five Freedoms between contracting nation states. That would have been a huge step forward in overcoming the artificial constraints imposed by national boundaries and sovereignty over airspace, but it would not have deconstructed the impact of national sovereignty in the way that the SEAM did. The SEAM moved beyond a multilateral Five Freedoms regime in two fundamentally important ways. Firstly, it relegated cabotage – reserving all domestic services for a country's own airlines – to the dustbin of history for Member States. Secondly, and a logical supplementary, was the creation of common establishment rights. So far as the Member States of the EU were concerned, among themselves there was no such thing any longer as a national airline, but only Community carriers with the same operating rights throughout the EU. The problem about how they operated outside the EU and obtaining foreign recognition for the concept of Community carrier was soon to tip the EU-US relationship into turmoil, but more of that later. The SEAM in other words reflected in regional form the definition that was provided in Chapter 4 of a globalized industry. That is with the caveats that it was regional and that it did not relate to the rest of the world in a way that was compatible with the concept at the heart of the globalization, namely a level playing field. But within the EU this is what now existed: a level playing field on which all players conducted themselves according to the same rules. This was not an economic laissez faire system. There were rules that made provision for commercially unviable routes justified on the grounds of social welfare and making the EU a coherent whole. There were competition rules, which safeguarded against dominant positions and predatory behavior; there were strict rules on emissions, noise pollution and compensation for passengers with delayed or cancelled flights; and so the list goes on. This was not a deregulated free market, but then neither was the aviation market in the US, though both were less regulated and more competitive than they had been. The US had led the way, but now the EU had moved ahead and presented a new model to the world to compete with the US Open-skies Model. How all this developed is the subject of the next chapter.

Notes

1 Remarks by Jeffrey N. Shane, Under Secretary for Policy, US Department of Transportation, International Aviation Club, Washington DC, 12 September 2006, text courtesy of EC Directorate of Transport and Energy (DG TREN previously DG VII).
2 'Civil Aviation Memorandum 2: Progress Towards the Development of a Community Air Transport Policy', COM(84)72, Final, 15 March 1984, p. i.
3 Australia and New Zealand have come closest to the SEAM as a model in the creation of their SAM and the ASEAN moved in the same direction with its own version of a SAM in 2015, http://www.aph.gov.au/binaries/house/committee/jsct/augustandsep tember2002/report/chapt6.pdf.
4 In 2016 Britain voted to leave the European Union, which places in serious question its continuing participation in the Single Market, including the SEAM. If BREXIT negotiations result in Britain's continuing access to the Single Market then there will be no change, but if not then Britain would be confronted with major issues of negotiating access not only to the SEAM, but also to the US market. Probably the likeliest scenario would be for the UK to become a member of the European Common Aviation Area, like Norway.
5 Ernst B. Haas, *Beyond the Nation State: Functionalism and International Organization*, Stanford: Stanford University Press, 1964; John Pinder, *Altiero Spinelli and the British Federalists: Writings by Beveridge, Robbins and Spinelli, 1937–43*, London: Federal Trust, 1998; Alan Milward, *The European Rescue of the Nation State*, 2nd edition, London: Routledge, 1999; Andrew Moravcsik, 'Preferences and Power in the European Community: A Liberal Intergovernmentalist Approach', *Journal of Common Market Studies* 31(iv), (1993), pp. 473–524.
6 The European Union came into being in 1993 succeeding the European Communities.
7 L. Gialloreto, *Strategic Airline Management: The Global War Begins*, London: Pitman Press, 1988; R. Pryke, *Competition among International Airlines*, Aldershot: Gower, 1987; S. Shaw, *Airlines and Management*, London: Pitman, 1985; H.A. Raben, 'Deregulation a Critical Interrogation', in H.A. Wassenbergh and H.P. van Fenema (editors), *International Air Transport: A Legal Analysis*, Deventer: Kluwer, 1981, pp. 1–24; R. Doganis, *Flying Off Course: The Economics of International Airlines*, London: Allen and Unwin, 1985.
8 Chartered airlines were important in providing cheap flights. The charter markets in Britain, Germany, Holland and Scandinavia were particularly well developed and charters accounted for 50% of the European aviation market in the mid-1970s. As

affinity requirements for charters became more and more flexible they constituted yet another pressure on the scheduled airlines to do something to bring prices down. See Dobson, *Flying in the Face of Competition*, chapters 4–6.

9   Treaty of Rome, 25 March 1957, preamble and Article 2.

10   *Ibid.*, Articles 2(f) and 74–84.

11   The following speak to the European airline industry to one degree or another: Dobson, *Globalization*; J. Erdmenger, *The European Transport Policy*, Aldershot: Gower, 1983; G. Majone (editor), *Deregulation or Re-Regulation? Regulatory Reform in Europe and the United States*, London and New York: Pinter and St. Martins, 1990; F. McGowan and C. Trengove, *European Aviation: A Common Market?* London: Institute for Fiscal Studies, 1986; P.P.C. Haanappel and G. Petsikas (editors), *EEC Air Transport Policy and Regulation and Their Implications for North America*, Deventer: Kluwer, 1989; P. Forsyth, 'Airline Deregulation in the United States: The Lessons for Europe', *Fiscal Studies* 4, (November 1983), pp. 7–21; S. Wheatcroft and G. Lipman, *Air Transport in a Competitive European Market: Problems, Prospects and Strategies*, London: Economist Intelligence Unit, Economist Publications Ltd., 1986; Pryke, *Competition among International Airlines*; D. O'Reilly and A.S. Sweet, 'The Liberalization and European Re-regulation of Air Transport', in W. Sandholtz and A.S. Sweet (editors), *European Integration and Supranational Governance*, Oxford: Oxford University Press, 1998, pp. 164–187; H. Stevens, *Transport Policy in the European Union*, Basingstoke: Palgrave, 2004; K. Button, K. Haynes and R. Stough, *Flying Into the Future: Air Transport Policy in the European Union*, Cheltenham: Edward Elgar, 1998.

12   Rome Treaty, Article 84(2).

13   Interview: official from DG IV, 22 May 1991. Regulation No. 17, 6 February 1962 and Regulation No. 141, 26 November 1962, *Official Journal of the European Community* (hereafter *OJ*), pp. L13/204 & L124/2751 respectively. On 19 July 1968 Regulation 1017 re-applied Regulation 17 to inland transport.

14   Case 167/73, Commission v. France, 1974 ECR, 359.

15   'Report on Competition in Intra-European Air Services', 1982, Paris, ECAC, CEAC Doc. No. 25.

16   Interviews, R. Fennes and F. Sorensen, 21 February 2000.

17   Sorensen Interviews, 21 February 2000 and 12 September 2001.

18   Gloria Garland, 'The American Deregulation Experience and the Use of Article 90 to Expedite EEC Air Transport Liberalisation', *European Competition Law Review*, 7, (1986), pp. 193–4.

19   Reasons have been given why IR theory has been eschewed here, but theoretical consideration about European integration can be simplified into a developing debate between inter-governmentalism, which argues that sovereign governments negotiate areas of integration while retaining national sovereign control, and various iterations of functionalism and institutionalism, which argue that they do not. The former school of thought is represented by Stanley Hoffmann, *The State of War: Essays on the Theory and Practice of International Politics*, New York: Praeger, 1965 and Moravcsik, *Preferences and Power in the European Community*, and the latter by David Mitrany, *A Working Peace System: An Argument for the Functionalist Development of International Organization*, London: Royal Institute for International Affairs, 1943, Haas, *Beyond the Nation State*, and W. Sandholtz and A. Stone Sweet, *European Integration*.

20   O'Reilly and Sweet suggest lobbying was significant for reform, but interview evidence from Commission officials suggests that the most powerful pressures that they felt from lobby groups was regulatory conservative. See O'Reilly and Sweet, 'The Liberalization and European Reregulation of Air Transport', Dobson, *Globalization and Regional Integration*, and J. Greenwood, *Interest Representation in the European Union*, Basingstoke: Palgrave, 2003.

21   Luxembourg Council 462nd Session 28/29 June 1977.

22 'European Airline Traffic after 1993', presentation by F. Sorensen, VII.C.1–839/90, 8 April 1991: copy courtesy of Sorensen.

23 Memorandum 1, 'Contributions of the EC to the Development of Air Transport Services', COM(79) 311, 6 July 1979, Supplement 5/79 EC Bulletin, 8139/79; Council Decision, 20 December 1979, 'Setting up a Consultation Procedure on Relations Between Member States and Third Countries in the Field of Air Transport and On Action Relating to Such Matters Within International Organizations', (80/50/EEC), No. L 18/24, 24 January 1980; Inter-Regional Services, OJ No. L 237, 26 August 1983; 'Progress Towards the Development of a Community Air Transport Policy', COM(84)72, 15 March 1984, otherwise known as Memorandum 2.

24 Sorensen Interview, 21 February 2000.

25 Loder Collection, Swansea University Library (hereafter Loder Collection), HE 9797A2, 'European Community: Commission Proposal for a Community Air Transport Policy', John Loder, UK Department of Transport, Analysis of Memorandum 2, September 1983.

26 White Paper 'Completing the Internal Market', COM(85)310, May 1985, paragraphs 109–10.

27 S. Williams, 'Internal Market and Common Market – the Single European Act versus the Treaty of Rome: Protectionism or Competitiveness in European Civil Aviation?', in P.P.C. Haanappel et al., *EEC Air Transport*, p. 19.

28 Loder Collection, HC 240.9, Statement by the Commission Representative at the 1006th session of the Council (Transport), 23 May 1985, 7087/85.

29 *Ibid.*, HC 240.9, John R. Steele, Note for the Attention of Mr. S. Clinton Davis, 29 April 1985, p. 1.

30 Cases 209–13/84, *Ministère public v. Lucas Asjes et al., Nouvelles Frontières*.

31 *Ibid.*, HC 240.9, 12 May 1986, Legal Service memorandum to Members of the Commission: Judgement Court of Justice 30 April 1986 Joined Cases 209 to 213/84, *Nouvelles Frontières*, p. 8.

32 *EC Bulletin* 1986–6, 2.1.233.

33 *Loder Collection*, HC 240.9, Draft letter, Sutherland for Commission to BA, undated.

34 Directives 87/601/EEC and 87/602/EEC; Regulations 3975/87 and 3976/87.

35 *Flight International*, 13 February 1988, 'Europe's New Rules: Substance or Illusion?', p. 9.

36 *EC Bulletin* 1987–12, 2.1.280.

37 *The Independent*, 31 July 1989, 'Sharing the Pie in the Sky'.

38 Stevens, *Op. Cit.* 1997, p. 30.

39 *Loder Collection* HC 240.9, Loder to Powell 1 December 1989.

40 *Ibid.* and Stevens, *Op. Cit.* 1997, pp. 32–3. Loder places the meetings at 13 and 14 not 15 and 16 November as in Stevens.

41 *Loder Collection* HC 240.9, Loder to Powell 1 December 1989.

42 *Ibid.*, HE 9762.5, Nicholas Argyris address to European Air Law Association, London, 27 July 1990.

43 *Ibid.*

44 Interview: senior official from the UK CAA, 23 May 2001.

45 Fennes Interview, 21 February 2000.

46 Stevens, *Op. Cit.*, 1997, pp. 33–4.

47 Interview: senior official DG IV, 22 February 2000.

48 Nicholas Argyris, 'EEC Competition Law Rules and Their Impact on Air Transport Services Ancillary Thereto', in Haanappel et al. (editors), *Op. Cit.*, p. 78.

49 *Flight International*, 7 November 1990, p. 12.

50 *Ibid.*

51 Remarks by Lord King, Royal Aeronautical Society 125th Anniversary Banquet, 16 May 1991.

52 Interview: senior official DG IV, 22 May 1991.
53 *Flight International*, 1 July 1992, 'EC Compromises on Air Competition', p. 6.
54 *Ibid.*, 21 July 1992, 'Not Liberal Enough?', p. 23.
55 'The Way Forward for Civil Aviation in Europe', COM(94)218 final, 1 June 1994, p. 3.
56 CAP 654, 'The Single European Aviation Market: Progress So Far', September 1995, UK CAA, London, p. vii.
57 *Financial Times*, 20 September 1995, 'Europe's Airlines', p. 21.
58 *Ibid.*
59 Dobson, *Flying in the Face of Competition*, pp. 180–86.
60 'Impact of the Third Package of Air Transport Liberalisation measures and European Commission Spokesman's Service', COM(96)415 final, 24 October 1996, 'Commission's report on impact of third and final stage of liberalisation from 1993–1996'.

6 Open-skies and a fully globalized world market

Challenge and reality 1992–2016

We are living through a period in which international aviation rules must change. Privatization, competition, and globalization are trends fuelled by economic and political forces that will ultimately prevail. Governments and airlines that embrace these trends will far outpace those that do not. The U.S. government will be among those that embrace the future.
Statement of United States International Air Transportation Policy, 3 May 1995[1]

Introduction: the focus and the challenge

While the Europeans moved gradually towards the SEAM, the US accelerated its own policy trajectory. In 1992 it struck the first Open-skies agreement. This was a turning point, but turbulent economic conditions in the wake of the Gulf War occasioned a temporary pause for reflection and caution on both sides of the Atlantic. In the US such caution was set aside in the 1995 Statement of Aviation policy, which reaffirmed Open-skies as the way forward, but in Europe the character of the European response to the recession was more equivocal and for a while seemed to belie hopes for liberalization.[2] How the situation played out in Europe, not just after the recession triggered by the First Gulf War but also after 9/11, was crucial for Europe and the emergence of a model fit for purpose for a truly global aviation market: this is the first focus of this chapter.

The second focus returns to areas which lie more in the technical than the commercial sphere, but nevertheless have significant economic consequences and are important for the creation of a fully globalized airline industry. They include most importantly air traffic control (ATC), allocation of scarce airport take-off and landing slots, and the bourgeoning impact of aviation-generated pollution.

The third focus is on the accelerating success of US Open-skies policy.

The fourth focus is on the US-EU negotiations for an open aviation area/ Open-skies agreement, which demonstrated that the US was now less willing than the EU to abandon nationally determined regulations that would continue to fracture and distort the market.

The European response to the Gulf War and 9/11

European airlines teetered on the brink of disaster. In February the AEA predicted 1990 would yield the first combined loss for its members for over a decade
as a result of spiraling costs, a depressed US market and the initial impact of the
Gulf crisis. Such losses paled to insignificance compared to what happened next.
When hostilities began traffic was hit catastrophically. Levels fell 25% within
two weeks. Load factors slumped to around 35%, which was over 15% down on
the same period a year before.[3] By April 1993 estimates of accumulated losses
for scheduled world airlines between 1990 and 1993 stood at $11.5 billion, with
European airlines accounting for nearly a half.[4] European airlines shed over
20,000 jobs: BA 9% of its workforce, KLM 12%, Sabena 18%, Iberia 10%, Ali-
talia's 8% and SAS 16%. In contrast Air France and Lufthansa strove to maintain
their work forces even though Air France, according to its Chairman Bernard
Attali, fell into massive deficit representing 5%, 12.5% and almost 50% of IATA
airlines' total deficits respectively in 1990, 1992 and 1993.[5] These grim figures
provided France and other regulatory conservative states with ammunition to
argue for slowing liberalization. They also provided the rationale for demanding
state aid.[6]

Transport Commissioner Karel Van Miert tried to head off the worst aspects
of protectionism, arguing that direct Community subsidies were not possible
and that the Commission could only offer financial help with infrastructure
improvements, but added, rather ominously for the liberal camp, that the Treaty
of Rome could be flexible where state action was concerned. The Commission appointed what became known as the *Comité des Sages* to make recommendations about what to do, which occasioned suspicions that the EU was
about to reverse direction on the SEAM. In any event such fears proved largely
unfounded.[7]

> The *Comité* firmly advises against any rollback of liberalisation. This would
> be inappropriate and self-defeating. It would render the global competitive-
> ness impossible.[8]

The report called for the full implementation of the three reform packages; however, there was a little more of the devil in the detail.

> The *Comité* reluctantly recognises the need for some states to act on a genu-
> ine "one time, last time" opportunity to put airlines on a normal commercial
> footing. The reasons for granting exceptions are essentially political.[9]

At least one could not fault the committee for its honesty, but in 1994 and 1995
the idea of flexibility stretched the credulity of many in the liberal camp as billions
of pounds of state aid poured into inefficient and some clearly unviable airlines.

State handouts were justified as one-off financial events that were supposed to
restructure the ailing airline in question and make it competitively fit and suitable
for privatization, though this latter possibility was not a compulsory requirement

State Aid 1991–1995 in £ million		
1991	Sabena	584
1992	Air France	665
1992	Iberia	670
1993	Aer Lingus	170
1994	Tap-Air Portugal	710
1994	Olympic Airways	995
1994	Air France	2400
1995	Iberia	445[10]

for receiving state aid. Instead of preparing airlines for competition, subsidies often simply seemed to featherbed them in their uncompetitive ruts, reward their inefficiency and grant them unfair advantages *vis-à-vis* other European airlines. Most galling of all for the liberalizers was that some airlines and governments seemed incapable of understanding what 'one' and 'last time' actually meant. The string of state aids and what appeared to be the weakness of the Commission were deeply troubling and disillusioning. And indeed difficulties with state ownership and state aids continued well beyond the spate of capital injections between 1991 and 1995. For example, Christian Blanc, in rather stark contrast to his predecessor Bernard Attali as head of Air France, resigned in September 1997 when the incoming socialist government reneged on previously given pledges on privatization that had been made in the wake of financial help for the airline. The new French government refused to proceed down the path of privatization.[11]

But, in fact, all that extravagant expenditure on inefficient state airlines in the 1990s sensitized many to the benefits of liberalization. Gaining state support for airlines was a Pyrrhic victory. As time passed, the Commission displayed a growing resolution, encouraged by British fulminations against subsidies, and a legal case brought by BM, BA, KLM and SAS to the European Court of Justice in 1994 against the Commission's approval of state aid for Air France. As one Brussels official put it at the time: 'If nothing else, this legal challenge is likely to stiffen the Commission's spine and toughen its attitude over future applications for state aid.'[12] It did. In the summer of 1998, when the Court declared the Commission's approval illegal, both Commissioners Van Miert and Neil Kinnock seemed rather pleased.[13] Attitudes to the whole issue of state aid gradually hardened. Parallel to the development of this hardening were gradual moves towards privatization. Such momentum stalled in France, but, by the end of the 1990s, KLM and Luxair had followed BA's path and become private companies, and state holdings in SAS, Lufthansa and Austrian Airlines had been reduced respectively to 50%, 52% and 52%. By March 1997 even someone as generally skeptical about European liberalization as Michael Bishop of BM felt able to say: 'We're seeing much greater scrutiny of state aid. It's not being squeezed out, but it will be over the next two or three years.'[14] His prediction was accurate. After the merger with KLM in 2004, privatization eventually took hold even in France with the government's shareholding dropping below 50%.

When the post 9/11 recession hit the airlines, the Commission to the surprise of many was less generous than US authorities. In the 12 months following, 9/11 the US government, in response to nearly $10 billion of losses and the shedding of 90,000 jobs in the US airline industry, provided $5 billion of cash aid and guarantees for $10 billion of loans. In 2002 Congress passed the Terrorism Risk Insurance Act by which the US government provided insurance cover to US airlines for terrorist attacks.[15] In contrast, the Commission was tired of its ailing airlines and, though the words were never publicly spoken, the post 9/11 recession was not altogether unwelcome. Many in DG TREN (DG VII) and the DG for Competition (DG IV) believed consolidation (a euphemism for mergers, take-overs and exits from the marketplace) was necessary if European airlines were to survive not just in Europe, but in the global marketplace.[16]

Soon after 9/11 *The Observer* reported the European Transport Commissioner, Loyola de Palacio, stridently insisting that there would be no 'government rescues for stricken airlines. There must be a shake-out of the industry, with weaklings going bust or being bought out and the stronger becoming bigger and taking on the world.' 'A market such as air transport is a global one, competing with the great US and Asian carriers. We need in Europe, also, world-size carriers which can compete.'[17] Some relief was forthcoming but European airlines were now experiencing a leaner regime.[18] They received less than their US counterparts and insufficient to prevent Sabena becoming the first Community flag carrier to disappear: it went into liquidation on 6 November with the last Sabena flight into Brussels on 7 November.[19] Later there were also mergers, the most important of which was KLM with Air France. The process of the demise or merger/takeover of state-owned national flag carriers in Europe had begun. This process had been deemed to be a political impossibility a bare 20 years before when liberalization began: both the ECAC COMPAS and the European Parliament Klinkenborg report had declared the political impossibility of a national flag carrier being allowed to fail or to be taken over by a rival.[20] They were wrong: state aids and the status and protection of national flag carriers were becoming phenomena of a bygone age. The airlines were gradually becoming just like any other commercial enterprise.

These were hugely important developments in Europe, because the US and Europe were at the time by far and away the most important players in the international civil aviation marketplace and they were now both on the liberalization track. But there were also other important developments within Europe that were technically outside the economic sector, but which had very important consequences for it and which also speak to the needs of a globalized industry.

Revisiting technical and safety matters

Change begets change and success begets new challenges and exposes existing deficiencies, and so it was with the metamorphosis of the airline industry as deregulation and liberalization played out on both sides of the Atlantic. How

ICAO and IATA laid the groundwork for the take-off of the industry by tending to technical and safety standards and facilitating ticketing and interlining has been explained in a previous chapter. Some of the issues that rose in profile in the 1960s and 1970s including terrorism have been touched on, but there were others that became pressing because of the very success of liberalization and industry expansion. These included global competition threatening job security, the rise in pollution from the vastly expanded aviation industry and emerging inadequacies of ground transport services, air traffic control and the number of take-off and landing slots at congested airports. There is insufficient space to deal fully with all these matters in detail but by saying a few words about ground transportation, air traffic control, slots and pollution the general point should emerge about the importance of consequential problems arising that need attention if the airline industry is to continue to thrive, grow and continue to move in the right direction. Sorting out such problems is a prerequisite if the industry is ever to become efficient, environmentally sustainable and fully globalized.

The proliferation and growth of regional routes in Europe as a result of the reform packages led to massive expansion of passenger numbers. This was notably so in the UK at airports such as Edinburgh, Birmingham, Luton, Stansted, East Midlands and Bristol, but with the notable exceptions of Birmingham and Stansted the ground transportation services to them were woefully inadequate. Between 2000 and 2014 Edinburgh Airport passenger numbers grew from 5 million to over 10 million a year, overcoming Glasgow's figures and making it Scotland's busiest airport.[21] Until 2014 access was by a dual/single carriageway road with some buses taking nearly half the time to travel from the airport to the city center as a plane takes from London to Edinburgh. The main railway line from Edinburgh to Aberdeen ran along the edge of the airport, but there was no provision for it to stop. In 2014 matters were improved by the opening of the Edinburgh tram network: other regional airports have not been so fortunate. If there cannot be rapid transit from airports to final destination it rather destroys the point of flying.

Speed and safety are also issues for ATC. In July 1992 Pieter Bouw of KLM claimed that ATC in Europe was 'the greatest source of concern for the European air transport industry.'[22] Delays in European airline operations in 1991 were 21% up on the previous year with an accumulated 106,000 hours of delays.[23] These were the result of a multiplicity of national ATC systems and technical dysfunctions, which compound the difficulty of creating efficient and world competitive airlines in Europe. This was symptomatic of the kind of fragmentation which was the antithesis of what a regional or globalized market should actually be. Over the last two and a half decades great strides forward have been made in improving ATC management in the SEAM, but in some cases serious problems not only abide, but are intensifying.

In 1961 EUROCONTROL was set up as an inter-governmental organization to try to meet the needs of scheduled international routes and overcome national parochialism, but it was pretty ineffective. A year before Bouw spoke out, Van Miert had bemoaned the lack of power in EUROCONTROL, the lack of political will among its members to do something effective about ATC and lack of effective participation by the EC. The Director General of EUROCONTROL, Keith Mack, responded with characteristic institutional defensiveness. He defended EUROCONTROL, opposed EC membership because it lacked the expertise required for effective action in this sphere and was over sanguine about EUROCONTROL's 1990 initiative, the European Air Traffic Control Harmonization and Integration Programme (EATCHIP). Working closely through ECAC, $3.6 billion were approved in March 1992 for the implementation stages of the program, but many in Europe were still profoundly dissatisfied with ATC arrangements.[24]

The *Comité des Sages* was particularly outspoken, deploring 'the lack of political willingness by the EU Council of Transport Ministers to tackle this ATC problem with the urgency needed.'[25] Something better than EATCHIP was needed because while it represented 'an essential step towards improving Europe's ATC system in a pragmatic way . . . there is no alternative to a truly Single European Air Traffic Management System.'[26]

The calls from the *Comité des Sages* went largely unheeded and only slow incremental reform took place for most of the 1990s. But then the pace picked up partly because of renewed moves by the EU to join EUROCONTROL, partly because of ATC problems exposed by the crisis in Kosovo and partly because of the vigor of the new Transport Commissioner Loyola de Palacio and the Commission's call for 'The Creation of the Single European Sky (SES)'.[27]

Action was desperately needed. Three hundred fifty thousand hours of flying time were now being wasted in Europe each year because of delays and non-optimal routing; however, not all of the delays were generated by ATC difficulties, as having to detour round blocked off military airspace was also a significant problem. The Commission's SES initiative garnered support in the Parliament and in the Council of Ministers. In November 2000 the High-Level Group appointed by the Council issued a report.[28] In its forward Commissioner Loyola de Palacio wrote of two overriding priorities:

> We face the challenge of organising the involvement of the military air traffic control service in the single sky. We will need the continued interest and support of the highest political authorities to build adequate structures that enable military air traffic authorities to gain confidence and to work closer together with their civilian counterparts. Second we must develop synergies with Eurocontrol as well as the Community's own capabilities to establish an agenda for reform and to implement changes.[29]

On 8 October 2002 the EU joined EUROCONTROL and this eased the way for closer cooperation and for more effective action. By 2003 EUROCONTROL was claiming that 'delays attributable to air traffic management have been virtually eliminated'.[30] This was an optimistic overstatement, but on 22 December 2003 a Memorandum of Cooperation covering implementation of the SES, research and development, data collection and analysis, satellite navigation, and international cooperation was signed. These developments, culminating in a new legal framework for the SES in 2004, have eased Europe's ATC problems in terms of delays. In 2004, with the fastest annual growth rate in traffic since 1999, delays were at an all-time low,[31] but costs were still high and there was still fragmentation and the need for more effective technology, standardization and better computer software.[32]

The EU has continued to make advances to improve the coherence and effectiveness of the system, harmonize technology through the SES Implementation Programme (SESAME), create a single framework and 'provide integrated seamless air traffic management.'[33] There is no doubt that concerted efforts by EUROCONTROL and the EU to improve traffic flows have met with substantial success, but as EUROCONTROL, itself, acknowledges:

> In spite of much effort to modernise and streamline it, Europe's air traffic management system remains safe but fairly costly. It is also hampered by heterogeneous working practices and constrained air route networks, which in the main, are based on national borders and not traffic air flows.[34]

Clearly some problems remained and further steps were taken in 2008 and 2013. The former resulted in the Single European Sky II and the latter the Single European Sky II+.[35] The Commission has wavered between optimism; for example DG TREN reported in 2005 that ATC development and reform were 'on track' to achieve the goals laid down in the Commission's 2001 White Paper on transport;[36] and in a more realistic appraisal, 'more is required to achieve full and timely compliance with SES legislation.'[37] The abiding problems are the illogicality – in aviation terms – of national boundaries, airspace blocked for military purposes, the interface between national ATC authorities, insufficient power and resources for the National Supervisory Authorities, the need for stronger performance reviews and a tangle of overlapping authority, which SESII+ promises to rationalize:

> Eurocontrol will focus on the operational issues (network manager), EASA [European Aviation Safety Agency] on technical rule drafting and oversight authority tasks, and the Commission on economic regulation.[38]

In 2012 there were 10.8 million minutes of Air Traffic Flow Management time lost, 7.8 million tons of unnecessary carbon dioxide emissions, €4.5 billion wasted because of flight inefficiencies and total unnecessary costs of €12.7 billion.[39] The rational efficiency potential for the SES remains only partially consummated and, while the European Parliament approved the SESII+ on 12 March 2014, problems obstructed further progress. At a time when the Members States needed to act in conjunction with the Commission over SESII+, exactly the opposite seemed to be happening as friction arose over implementing functional airspace blocs (FABs) that would transcend national boundaries. With only two FABs in place in northern Europe, the Commission suspended infringement procedures, but the damage had already been done. Movement for further developing the SES seemed to one aviation journal to have 'deviated' and run onto a 'zigzag path'.[40] After moving successfully in the right direction, the SES now seems to be in trouble. A globalized industry would have the same challenges only writ larger.

The need to ration landing slots is a symptom of success. It is also a problem that distorts competition and can be used as a form of protectionism by excluding would-be newcomers and this again applies not only in Europe but globally. The problems are complex. An airline that has built up a bloc of slots, which enable it to operate effectively in terms of assembling and distributing passengers, is understandably loath to release any of them when that might compromise its optimum operating efficiency. This is a classic case where the whole is more than the sum of its parts. Take one or more parts away and they have an incommensurately negative impact on performance. That factor has been recognized by 'grandfather' rights: past use justifies present possession. However, such rights can be abused. An airline might not need a number of slots, but might be reluctant to release them for fear of competition from a new entrant to the market. Such new entrants furthermore cannot usually succeed commercially without a critical mass of slots at an airport, which enable effective assembly and distribution of passengers. Trying to distribute scarce slots equitably in these circumstances is difficult. It has either to be done by market forces, but then there is always the possibility of airlines with deep pockets buying up slots simply to pre-empt competition, or by deploying some criteria to determine how they can be distributed fairly. Another option of course, for easing the situation, is to expand the infrastructure and create more slots. In 1993, in the opinion of Virgin Atlantic's founder Richard Branson:

> The clearest demonstration of the nature of barriers to new entrants is to be found in the rules governing the allocation between airlines of airport take-off and landing slots in Europe.[41]

Until the Commission entered this fraught area of airline operations, the world's slot allocation regime was coordinated through IATA and its Scheduling Guidelines, which essentially worked in favor of the major scheduled airlines and helped to consolidate their dominance through grandfathering. At congested airports this created a major entry obstacle for new competitors and restricted expansion of in-place existing smaller airlines. Under pressure from liberalizers, IATA modified its guidelines marginally in 1991 in order to give more priority to new entrants, but this was only a placatory nod in their direction. The Commission struggled to introduce a more liberal regime in Package 3, but implacable opposition forced abandonment. Nevertheless, negotiations continued and by the end of 1992 the Commission succeeded in getting the Council of Ministers to approve Regulation 95/93.[42]

The Regulation required Member States to designate congested airports and appoint an independent coordinator to apply legally binding rules for slot allocations. This regime, while a step forward, was not radical: the Commission recognized it was only possible to tweak at the margins of the problem. It set 'out common rules aimed at ensuring neutral, transparent and non-discriminatory decisions on the allocation of slots at congested airports.'[43] Once an airport was designated as 'fully coordinated', then any slot not utilized 80% of the time would be tossed into a pool for reallocation by the coordinator. Up to 50% of that pool would then be reallocated to new entrants. Unfortunately the pools remained small and populated by unwanted off-peak slots. A new entrant was defined as an airline with less than 2% or 3% respectively of an airport or airport system's daily slots. The essential point was that the new regime only released a modest amount of unattractive slots for reallocation and new entrants soon lost their privileged status. In short, problems abided: as Virgin Express executive Jonathan Ornstein complained in 1997 it was still difficult to get slots at Brussels airport even though it was 'an airport where you can fire a canon down the runway most of the time without hitting anything.'[44]

Regulation 95/93 had only had minor impact, but reports on and debate about the problem continued with dire warnings from defenders of the *status quo*.[45] Karl-Heinz Neumeister of the AEA emphasized the extent of potential damage if there were a 'gradual withdrawal of grandfather rights, exclusion of alliance partners from new entrant status, and confiscation of slots held by incumbent carriers.'[46]

By the time the Commission made proposals to the Council of Ministers to amend Regulation 95/93 in 2001 it was clear that radical change was yet again not possible. Unfortunately, the Commission could find little that was politically acceptable for solving any of the substantial problems that afflicted the distribution of slots. On 21 April 2004 the Council finally promulgated Regulation 793/2004 to replace 95/93. It did little to improve the situation and marginally less than the Commission had asked for.[47] Differences among the Member States and between them and the Commission and the essentially intractable nature of the problem of slots severely limited what could be done. Officials at DG TREN in September 2006 observed that the number of slots coming under the auspices of the reallocation rules was still only a small percentage of the slots needed by airlines seeking better competitive positions and that the Commission continued to struggle to find a better solution to the problem.

In 2012 there were further developments in the European Parliament and the Council following on from a Proposal from the Commission for a Regulation on Common Rules for the Allocation of Slots at European Union Airports (Recast).[48] It was now accepted that there could be a secondary market in slots, meaning that they could be bought and sold subject to safeguards against abuse by airlines with deep pockets. This is simply permissive not a requirement and so far a secondary market has only developed in the UK. The proposal also broadened the definition of 'new entrant' to the market to try to enhance the possibility for them to retain their preferential status longer and thus garner more slots. The level of use for grandfather rights was raised from 80% to 85% and the time frames, during which these requirements applied for the peak and off-peak seasons, were expanded. All this was with the intention of loosening up the market in slots, but these proposals have still not yet been passed and slots remain a difficult and contentious issue. For example, there is a long-standing and ongoing dispute between Germany on the one hand and Emirates and Etihad airlines on the other concerning the difficulty of those airlines gaining slots at German airports. One difficult aspect of this for Lufthansa is that Emirates and Etihad are both based in the United Arab Emirates (UAE) and as such can offer no significant market opportunity to Germany in return for access to the German/EU market. But in addition to this there are concerns in Germany, as well as in France and the US, that Emirates and Etihad receive huge subsidies, which unfairly advantage them in the international marketplace.[49] In these circumstances slot allocations can be used either – depending on one's perspective – to help level the competitive playing field or for protection.

Slots illustrate an interesting problem. Their scarcity is a symptom of success, though others would argue it is also the result of insufficient investment in infrastructure and there is obvious truth in that. But there are also huge problems to do with noise and emissions pollution, which make it very difficult to expand airports such as Heathrow. Slots are a technical, or infrastructure, issue but they have a direct and important impact on the competitive potential of the industry. Slots not only symbolize industry success, they also epitomize complexity in the industry in the way that they impact on efficiency and competitiveness and how solutions might be found in various ways: by the creation of secondary slot markets; through developing criteria for equitable distribution of slots; and by expanding the infrastructure. These three approaches are of course not mutually exclusive and indeed the Member States, the EU, airports and airlines have deployed all three approaches. The ironic and disappointing fact is however that they have only had modest success.

For a globalized market, defined as a regime in which all world airlines operate according to the same rules and conditions, tackling such problems is vital. Krishna R. Urs, US Deputy Assistant Secretary for Transportation, insisted in a speech in Beijing in 2011: 'we must work to ensure that potential new barriers like slots availability, airspace congestion, noise restrictions, and environmental levies do not undermine the hard won liberalization achieved through our open skies agreements.'[50] He was correct, but balancing the benefits of affordable and efficient air travel and the costs to health and climate change of aviation pollution is hugely challenging and an issue that has increasingly loomed large over the last three decades. European Commission President Jose Manuel Barroso, in November 2006, highlighted the problem of global warming and declared the intention of making the EU the world pioneer of green issues.[51] This was not new for the Commission. In its 2001 White Paper it argued in favor of 'environmentally favourable' modes of transport and that 'air traffic must therefore be brought under control.'[52] Estimates by the Intergovernmental Panel on Climate Change in its report 'Aviation and the Global Atmosphere' indicated that aviation contributed 3.5% to global climate change in 1992.[53] But since then, the airline industry has expanded massively. In 2003–2004 alone there was a rise of 8.9 million passengers in Britain on scheduled flights. Many believe that the planet, never mind Europe, cannot sustain this level of unrestrained activity in the airline market and the most recent report on aviation pollution in Europe does not make comforting reading.

Between 1990 and 2005 carbon dioxide emissions from aircraft in Europe rose by 80%. 'However, due to technological improvements, fleet renewal, increased ATM [air traffic management] efficiency and the 2008 economic downturn, both emissions and noise exposure in 2014 are around the same levels.'[54] Unfortunately the likely increase between 2014 and 2035 is estimated to be 43% and this is within the framework of the EU, one of the most progressive in terms of sensitivity towards and action to limit climate change. The future of aviation has a problem and a challenge, but it is not alone. Placing aviation in the wider context of overall pollution puts things into perspective. In 2012 aviation contributed about 13% of all EU transport and 3% of total EU carbon dioxide emissions. Figures for aviation nitrogen emissions are on a more worrying trend, as they have quadrupled relative to other sources of nitrogen pollution since 1990, but are similar to carbon emissions in quantity, namely about 14% of all transport generated.[55] Overall the picture does not provide grounds for complacency. Pollution and climate change must be addressed and addressed with more vigor and resources than has been the case to date and the aviation industry must play its part in reducing pollution, but it is difficult to see why aviation should be treated as a category apart from other major polluters. Having said that, it is the case that aviation pollution presents a problem as equally difficult and intractable as the problems spawned by air sovereignty, namely cabotage and ownership and control, which have compromised the chances for efficient airline market operations.

The US and the Open-skies strategy 1992–2007

US 'Open-skies policy' means free pricing and route access, capacity and frequency determined commercially by market demand. It provides unrestricted Third, Fourth, Fifth and Sixth Freedom rights, unless there are constraints because of a scarcity of take-off and landing slots. The US has also combined its Open-skies policy with the offer of antitrust immunity to airline alliances. Possible levels of collaboration in an alliance range from simple interlining and shared frequent flier programs to merger-like cooperation of a joint venture. This is an integral aspect of US Open-skies policy and was one of the main inducements for other countries to enter such agreements because alliances help to overcome the problem of assembling and distributing passengers at international gateways in large domestic markets such as that of the US, otherwise protected by cabotage and national ownership and control laws. Alliances allow the domestic and regional operations of one partner to distribute and assemble passengers in connection with the long-haul operations of the other on a reciprocal basis through code-sharing agreements or by otherwise dovetailing operations.

The US had great success with Open-skies: it struck 10 agreements in 1995 with European countries and notably added Germany to its portfolio the year after. France succumbed in 2001 and the UK in 2007 through the EU-US

Aviation Agreement. US airlines finally had more access to Heathrow and, between 2008–2010, US departures from there rose by 15.3% in the context of a contracting overall transatlantic market. By 2016 the US had 119 Open-skies agreements worldwide.[56] Of the 14 countries that currently have airlines carrying over 50 million passengers a year, only China and Russia have not concluded Open-skies agreements with the US. Once again the US was leading the world airline system forward to lower cost flights delivered in a more seamless and efficient way.[57] The international airline regime was closer than it ever had been to a globalized and more uniform marketplace that operated largely on commercial lines.

But, the industry still suffered from varying *modus operandi* ranging from the EU SEAM, which abolished cabotage and national ownership and control laws; through the similarly liberal EU-Canadian agreement; the 1996/2000 Australian-New Zealand Single Air Market (SAM), which, while very liberal, retains national control regulations; to the US and ASEAN (Association of South East Asian Nations) Open-skies regimes, and the more protectionist practices of countries such as Russia and China.[58] Furthermore, notwithstanding its championing of liberalization, there were and still are anomalies in the position of the US. The first of these has to do with an integral part of its Open-skies strategy: alliances.

The US Department of Transportation has credited alliances with bringing fares down on transatlantic routes, increasing passenger numbers faster than non-alliance operators, creating greater efficiencies and delivering more seamless travel. 'The "Alliance Network Effect" will therefore play a key role in the evolving international aviation economic and competitive environment.'[59] But are alliances the optimal solution to the residual fragmentation that still exists even in liberalized Open-sky markets? Is there not a better solution?

Prima facie, alliances would appear to epitomize old cartel-type operations and hence anticompetitive practices. From the perspective of the Commission, the picture was not quite so rosy as the US Department of Transportation liked to paint. There had always been concerns in Europe about the market being allowed to have its way, especially if that led to dominant positions. In 1990 Nicholas Argyris of DG IV urged the need for 'effective safeguards against anti-competitive behaviour' in the same breath that he noted that since 1978 the US authorities have not opposed 'a single merger'.[60] By September 2001, alliances were causing real concern in the Commission. The Star Alliance 'is virtually squeezing out other US carriers' and 'was reducing or eliminating competition in a large part of the European market.' At the time Austrian Airlines was looking for a new alliance partner and was eventually drawn into the Star Alliance. The Commission would have much preferred it to join the Oneworld Alliance, but as one senior European official remarked: 'we cannot say it.'[61]

By 2010, however, there appeared to be some convergence in European and American thinking on alliances with a more favorable attitude towards them prevailing amongst Commission members, albeit with some significant caveats. Following the 2007 EU-US Aviation Agreement, and in particular the provisions of Annex 2 for collaboration between regulatory authorities, the US Department of

Transportation and the Commission jointly published a report on alliances and expressed the view that 'The global alliance strategy is rooted in the fundamentals of network economics and a global economy.'[62] Additionally:

> Since ownership and control restrictions will remain to limit the freedom of carriers to merge and given that alliances result in significant benefits for carriers, global alliances and immunised JVs [joint ventures] . . . [alliances] seem likely to continue to play an important role in transatlantic markets.[63]

In short, given the *de facto* existence of cabotage and national ownership and control laws, alliances were the best way of dealing with the barriers they created in the marketplace. As will become clear when the negotiations for the 2007 EU-US Aviation Agreement are considered in the next section, this *de facto* state of affairs was not just a given, it was a political choice and one the Europeans preferred not to make. The SEAM for example had done away with cabotage and national ownership and control. If that were done more widely: Whither airline alliances then? But this is to anticipate later arguments.

Market improvements and greater choice for consumers, after Open-skies was applied to Heathrow in the wake of the 2007 agreement, seemed to support claims about the benefits of Open-skies and alliances. However, the transatlantic is dominated by the three mega-alliances: Star, Oneworld and Skyteam, which in 2010 respectively held 37.6%, 22.7% and 28.3% of the market, amounting to nearly 90% of the total. Since the implementation of the EU-US Air Transport Agreement, key players in the alliances deepened cooperation to what the US Department of Transport and the Commission term 'joint venture levels', such as in the Oneworld Alliance between American Airlines, BA and Iberia. Competition authorities on both sides of the Atlantic are sensitive to such developments and keep an eye on the effects on competition:

> In markets where there is potential competitive harm, the authorities have generally tried to alleviate it with tailor-made remedies. The authorities agree to give consideration to adopting remedies that are proportional to the competitive harm that has been identified as resulting from the proposed transaction.[64]

So the effects of alliances are clearly not always positive or competition inducing and whether countermeasures are sufficient remains moot. For example, recent research indicates that non-member airlines reduced their traffic to alliance partners' hub airports on transatlantic routes by 4.1–11.5%.[65] In such cases the trade off with consumer benefits, which alliances deliver, continues to justify their existence, but reduced competition is inevitable. This is a very difficult area for regulatory authorities balancing competition and consumer benefits, but more importantly, the jury is still out on the key question as to whether alliances are the best solution to the residual fragmentation that still exists in liberalized Open-sky markets.

The second anomaly in the US's position was that even after deregulation there was never a free market. US airlines in difficulties are allowed Chapter 11 protection under which they can operate under favorable terms while seeking to regain financial viability.

The third anomaly is that the CRAF allows the US government in times of crisis to call upon US civil airlines for up-lift capacity to transport troops abroad and in return the Fly America Program reserves all official government air travel for US airlines (though this has now been modified by the EU-US agreement).

And the fourth anomaly is that the US has traditionally prohibited wet leasing of foreign aircraft (i.e. aircraft supplied with their own foreign crews). But all these rather specific matters pale to insignificance when set against US cabotage and ownership and control laws, which restrict foreign access to the US domestic market.

Of course, cabotage and ownership and control laws traditionally apply in all other countries as well, but this is such a significant issue regarding the US domestic airline market because it is so huge. To grasp just how huge there needs to be both comparators and absolute figures. In 2012 US domestic and international airlines carried 743,096,000 passengers. That was almost equivalent to the combined passenger total of the next five countries' airlines all put together, namely, in descending order, those of China, the UK, Japan, Germany and Brazil. In 2013 of the total 743.1 million passengers carried by US airlines 645.6 million were domestic carriage.[66] It is that huge domestic proportion of total US airline enplanements and the relative size of the US passenger market to the global market that makes US cabotage so unique and so important with regard to creating a level competitive playing field for international civil aviation.

This was the state of play in the international airline system and in the development of US policy when the EU brought about a crisis that forced the US and the EU speedily to re-negotiate their aviation relationship. And those talks while reaching an agreement also exposed a growing difference of outlook.

The possibility of a transatlantic open aviation area[67]

Open-skies ASAs were inconsistent with Community law – specifically because they recognized the concept of national rather than Community carriers – and they challenged the spirit of a unified EU market and the concept of a level playing field by granting some Member States commercial operating rights to the US, which were not available to others. As a result of such considerations and with the ambition of gaining control over the negotiation of external aviation relations for itself, the Commission brought suit at the European Court of Justice against eight member countries challenging the legality of their ASAs with the United States. The Court ruled in 2002 that the 'nationality clauses' of the ASAs were a violation of community law. This threatened turmoil over the Atlantic and pushed the two sides into negotiations for an EU-US ASA to supersede the existing national ASAs between the Member States and the US.[68] Talks began in June 2003.

There was a long-standing tradition of the US being the *demandeur* for open markets and increased competition and Europe being at best a recalcitrant responder; however, the tables were now turned. The EU proposed an Open Aviation Area that went way beyond US Open-skies. First and immediately most important of all for the EU, the US was asked to recognize EU airlines as Community and not national carriers. This would allow them to operate from any point in the EU to any point in the US and overcome the legal problem that threatened turmoil. But this was not all. The EU also proposed merging US and EU cabotage and removing foreign ownership and control restrictions. Finally, the EU called for harmonization of competition and safety regulations so as to attain a fully integrated market. In other words this was the European SEAM writ large to embrace the US.

In preparing the ground for the talks the EU commissioned the US-based Brattle Group to analyze the economic effects of an open aviation area (OAA). Its findings epitomized the kind of benefits to be reaped from liberalization, which the USA had long argued for.

- Annual transatlantic passenger numbers would increase from 4 million to 11 million, meaning that transatlantic travel as a percentage of total global air travel would increase by 9% to 24%;
- Intra-EU air travel would also increase significantly, to 35.7 million passengers per year, an increase of 13.6 million;
- Consumer benefits of $5.2 billion would be created annually as a direct result of increased competition, lower fares and increased passenger numbers;
- Finally, the report concluded that directly related industries would experience an increase in economic output of $3.6 billion per year, taking the total to $8.1 billion per year.[69]

The question was, would the Americans stay true to their long-standing position or would their liberalism give way to the forces of economic protectionism partly informed by what many saw as spurious political and security concerns?

There was little US opposition to the concept of Community carrier and so the US conceded this early in the negotiations. Otherwise, however, the OAA was much farther than the US was prepared to go and that requires some detailed explanation to demonstrate just how politically fraught international aviation issues remain.

Strong opposition by US airlines, labor organizations and some sections of the Congress made cabotage essentially a dead issue from the start. Realizing this the Commission negotiators switched their attention to ownership and control. But changes here were also strongly opposed by pilot and airline industry labor organizations. In addition, the issue was complicated by national security considerations. There was some fear that if airlines in the US came under foreign control the CRAF might be compromised, or at least that the use of the aircraft could become complicated by political considerations. The Commission reluctantly in the light of all this realized that changes to ownership and control laws would be impossible during the presidential election year of 2004. Consequently, they took to the Transport Ministers a draft agreement in which the only major concession was US recognition of Community carriers. The EU Transport Council rejected this as insufficient and sent the negotiators back to get movement on ownership and control, wet leasing, CRAF and the Fly America Program.

US Secretary of Transportation Norman Mineta was furious and negotiations did not resume until 2005. Then EU negotiators were surprised to receive signals that movement on ownership and control might be possible. Mineta intimated that, while changing the law would not be possible, a reinterpretation of the statute by the Department of Transportation using a notice of proposed rule-making (NPRM) could provide some room for liberalization. Traditionally the concept of control had been interpreted very strictly in the US, but the likelihood of change turned out to be a false hope. Statutory law had evolved through court decisions, which were then incorporated by Congress into law in ways that made the reinterpretation of statutory provisions very difficult and highly vulnerable to legal challenge.[70]

In any case before the Department of Transportation could rise from the starting blocks it suffered from a firestorm of political opposition to the NPRM. Airline labor unions and pilots associations opposed it out of fear of job losses. Because of the influence of their labor constituents, both Democratic Senator Daniel Inouye, Chairman of the Senate Committee on Commerce, Science and Transportation, and Democratic Representative James Oberstar, Chairman of the House Transportation and Infrastructure Committee, strongly opposed the measure. The personal friendship of Senator Inouye with Republican Senator Ted Stevens, Vice Chairman of the Senate Committee on Commerce, Science and Transportation, assured that the Chairman would have the Vice Chairman's support.[71] Against such formidable Congressional opposition, the Department of Transportation did not have the status and clout to make the NPRM stick without strong pressure from the White House. However, this issue was not perceived as having high enough priority for the president to expend political capital to ensure a satisfactory reinterpretation of the statute.

Further complicating the issue was a conflagration of political opposition that burst forth in 2006 after a Dubai company, DP Ports, purchased a British company, Pacific and Orient, that was managing six major US ports and a number of smaller ones. US Coast Guard intelligence officials raised some concerns about the national security implications of having US ports managed by a Dubai firm and several US politicians rose up in chorus opposing the deal. Public opinion was easily incited against the idea as well. While the NPRM was in no way related to the ports issue, those opposed to the NPRM could in the prevailing climate easily argue that, on national security grounds, even the commercial aspects of US airlines should not be under the control of foreigners.

In addition to all of these complications, Continental Airlines maneuvered strategically to oppose the NPRM. Continental at the time was not party to an immunized alliance (i.e. granted antitrust immunity). Unlike other American airlines, such as United, it would not be able to juggle take-off and landing slots at

Heathrow Airport under a liberalized regime with alliance partners. Continental would only be able to get slots if it were possible to buy them. European Commission rules regarding the trading of landing slots in a secondary market were vague until clarified in 2012; however, slots were regularly traded at Heathrow well before that and sanctioned by the British High Court.[72] Once Continental was able to purchase slots at Heathrow it dropped its opposition.

In the meantime, however, the Department of Transportation had backtracked. It stated that any delegation of authority to foreigners to make decisions concerning commercial policy of a US airline would have to be revocable.[73] That created uncertainty and effectively undercut any prospect of foreign investment. In any case, the statement of clarification did little to mollify political opposition to the NPRM, so, shortly after the election of a Democratic majority in both houses of Congress in the mid-term elections in November 2006, the Department of Transportation withdrew its proposal.

Even though the EU Transport Ministers had said that changes in US foreign investment and control regulations were essential, in the end they relinquished such demands and struck agreement. The US recognized Community carriers and made other minor concessions including on cargo and Seventh Freedom rights (the right to commercial carriage between two states, neither of which is the airline's country of origin), and on some modifications to the Fly America Program. But a limit of 25% on foreign-owned voting stock and a prohibition of any semblance of 'actual control' remained. In return the US achieved its last remaining major goal in Europe – access to Heathrow Airport through EU acceptance of Open-skies. It had conceded little in return apart from recognition of EU Community carriers and now only had matters of marginal concern in Europe for any future talks.

The agreement was essentially traditional Open-skies and fell a long way short of what the EU proposed. The British, bitter about the opening of Heathrow and lack of concessions on ownership and control, insisted on a provision in the agreement that in the Stage 2 negotiations, which began in May 2008, unless the US agreed to changes in its policies regarding foreign ownership and control, the EU would have the right to withdraw from the agreement. That, as the Americans knew full well, was an empty threat because it would tip everyone back to the original situation, namely the illegal status of European ASAs. In 2010 the second-round negotiations were concluded and again the US did not move on ownership and control. There was little incentive for them to do so as there was nothing of real importance that they needed from the Europeans.

On 24 June 2010, a protocol to amend the first-stage EU-U.S. Air Transport Agreement was signed and entered into provisional application. The protocol did not remove the foreign ownership and control restrictions. Both sides did commit to the shared goal of removing market access barriers to maximize benefits, including enhancing the access of airlines to the global capital markets, and the development of a process of cooperation in this regard.[74]

This was not a single aviation market. It did not meet the criteria for a model of a globalized aviation industry because the playing field was still not level. The distortions of cabotage and ownership and control laws prevented that, and alliances, at least in the views of the more radical, only ameliorate such distortions while posing serious problems of their own. The hope that the EU and the US might create a single transatlantic market of critical mass, which would draw in others in a process that could lead to a fully globalized world aviation market, was lost.

Conclusion

International civil aviation has travelled a long way since the early part of the twentieth century and the rate of change accelerated remarkably during the last quarter century. For a while it looked as if the impact of the First Gulf War might unravel the onward march of liberalization of the industry, especially in Europe, but while it caused setbacks it did not result in a long-term reversal of developments. If anything the Gulf War acted as a catalyst that was re-charged by the aftermath of 9/11 for moving Europe away from state subsidies and propping up commercially unviable airlines. Meanwhile in the US, after serious difficulties, the momentum to expand the number of Open-skies agreements gathered pace again.

The changes wrought by the new dispensation that had emerged first in the US and spread to Europe in the guise of the SEAM helped to create a more efficient and larger international airline market, but that in turn raised challenges such as in the field of airport access, ATC, the allocation of scarce take-off and landing slots at airports and pollution. Over time technology has done much to ease many of these types of problems, including security issues, but others abide and continue to cause dysfunctions in operations and fair competition. As ever, it is in those areas that raise national political concerns that have proven to be the most intractable.

Emerging out of all these changes came a possible chance to take yet another step towards a more globalized industry operating on a level playing field when the European Court of Justice precipitated talks between the EU and the USA in 2002–2003. In terms of the development of the international civil aviation industry, the two issues at the heart of those talks that could have re-crafted the international airline system were: Would the US join with the EU in merging cabotage and abandoning national ownership and control regulations with a view to creating a transatlantic aviation area whose operating regime would be comparable to the one that then currently applied in the SEAM? And furthermore, would the creation of such an Atlantic aviation area be of sufficient critical mass to draw in others morphing the regional Atlantic market into a truly global market? As we have seen the answer to the first question was negative, which left the second redundant. All this left a third question hanging: What might come next?

Notes

1 *US Federal Register*, Department of Transportation, 'Statement of the United States International Air Transportation Policy', 3 May 1995, 60 FR 21841.
2 *Ibid.*

3 *Flight International*, 13 February 1991, 'European Airlines Declare 1990 Losses', p. 12.

4 *Ibid.*, 20 January 1993, Airline Apocalypse', p. 25 and 28 April 1993, 'Aerospace Apocalypse', p. 26.

5 H-L. Dienel and P. Lyth (editors), *Flying the Flag: European Commercial Air Transport Since 1945*, Basingstoke: Macmillan, 1998, pp. 40–1.

6 Not everyone saw the crisis as inimical to liberalization's prospects: *Flight International* observed that the 'Gulf War provides many with an excuse to slim down ready to compete when growth returns.' *Flight International*, 20 February 1991, 'Where Have All the Airline Jobs Gone?', p. 22.

7 *Ibid.*, 21 July 1993, 'Twelve Wise Men', pp. 22–3.

8 *Expanding Horizons: A Report by the Comité des Sages for Air Transport to the European Commission*, January 1994, p. 17.

9 *Ibid.*, p. 21.

10 Handley Stevens, *Liberalisation of Air Transport in Europe: A Case Study in European Integration*, London: European Institute, LSE, 1997, p. 44, citing 'Aviation State Aid' briefing by UK Department of Transport, 5 October 1995, similar figures except expressed in ecus may be found in Button et al., *Flying into the Future*, p. 69.

11 *Flight International*, 10 September 1997, 'Blanc Quits Over Privatisation', p. 12.

12 *Financial Times*, 10 November 1994, 'Struggle at the Airport Gates', p. 22.

13 *Aerospace International*, August 1998, p. 7.

14 *Financial Times*, 11 March 1997, 'Freedom to Go a Little Crazy', p. 19.

15 *The Observer*, 22 September 2002, 'Airlines Fear Gathering Storm', *Business* p. 4; *Aerospace International*, October 2001, 'Airlines Suffer', p. 8.

16 Interviews with three Commission officials, one from DG TREN (previously DG VII), and two officials from the DG for Competition (formally DG IV), both conducted 25 September 2006.

17 *The Observer*, 23 September 2001, 'EU Wants Shake-Outs, Rather than Hand-Outs', *Business*, p. 4.

18 *Aerospace International*, July 2002, p. 4; not surprisingly Air France was compensated beyond the four-day compensation period and later investigated by the Commission.

19 *The Guardian*, 'Belgian Airline Goes Bust with Loss of 12,000 Jobs', 8 November 2001.

20 *COMPAS Report* 1982, p. 47; Report of the Committee on Transport of the European Parliament on Memorandum 2 of the Commission, the *Klinkenborg Report*, PE Doc A2–86/85/A, 7 August 1985.

21 www.edinburghairport.com and 'UK Civil Aviation Authority Summary of Activity at UK Airports 2000', www.caa.co.uk, both retrieved 20 February 2015.

22 *Flight International*, 15 July 1992, 'Airlines Dissatisfied with European ATC', p. 9.

23 *Ibid.*

24 *Ibid.*, 31 July 1991, 'EC Wants EUROCONTROL Changes', p. 6; and 25 March 1992, 'Second-Course EATCHIP Cleared by ECAC', p. 10.

25 *Expanding Horizons*, p. 23.

26 *Ibid.*

27 'The Creation of the Single European Sky', COM(1999)614 final, 1 December 1999.

28 European Commission Directorate-General Energy and Transport, 'Single European Sky: Report of the High-Level Group', Brussels, November 2000.

29 *Ibid.*, pp. 3–4.

30 *Aerospace International*, July 2003, 'Clear the Skies', p.14.

31 www.cfmu.eurocontrol.int/cfmu/g . . .

32 EC Regulations Nos. 549/2004, 550/2004, 551/2004 and 552/2004, effective 20 April 2004.

33 *Aerospace International*, January 2003, p. 4, and EC Regulations Nos. 549/2004, 550/2004, 551/2004 and 552/2004.

34 EUROCONTROL, 'The Single European Sky', www.eurocontrol.int/ses/public/stand ard_page/sk_ses.html.

34 *Ibid.*

35 SESII proposed June 2008, COM(2008)389 Single European Sky II adopted November 2009 Regulation (EC) No. 1070/2009 of 21 October 2009; SESII+ proposal COM(2013)0410.

36 *Assess: Assessment of the contribution to TEN and other transport measures to the mid-term implementation of the White paper on European Transport Policy for 2010*, Transport and Mobility Leuven, 28 October 2005 for DG TREN, Annex XIV, p. 28.

37 'Report from the Commission to the European Parliament and the Council on the Implementation of the Single Sky Legislation: Time to Deliver', COM(2011)731 final, 14 November 2011.

38 COM(2013)0410.

39 IATA Fact Sheet: Single European Sky, December 2014, www.iata.org/pressroom/ facts_figures/fact_sheets/Pages/ses.aspx, retrieved 19 February 2015.

40 *Aviation Week and Space Technology*, 27 February 2015, www.aviationweek.com, retrieved 19 September 2016.

41 Richard Branson, Address to the IEA Conference, 6 October 1993. He delivered something similar to the European Aviation Club in Brussels a few days later, reported in *Flight International*, 20 October 1993, with headline, 'Branson Rages at Europe', p. 12.

42 Council Regulations (EEC) No. 95/93, 18 January 1993 and No. 1617/93, 1 July 1993.

43 *Expanding Horizons*, p. 20.

44 *Financial Times*, 11 March 1997, 'Freedom to Go a Little Crazy', p. 19.

45 Coopers and Lybrand, 'Application and Possible Modification of Council Regulation 95/93 on Common Rules for the Allocation of Slots at Community Airports', 17 October 1995.

46 AEA Information, undated, reporting on Neumeister speech 'Better Use of Airport Slots in the EU', Düsseldorf, Hochtief AirPort Symposium, 17 September 2001.

47 A report for DG TREN claimed that the reform only had 'limited institutional impact', ASSESS: *Assessment of the contribution of the TEN and other transport policy measures to the mid-term implementation of the White Paper on the European Transport Policy for 2010*. Transport and Mobility Leuven, 28 October 2005. Annex XIV, Qualitative Analysis of Air Transport Issues.' Commission of the European Communities White Paper 12 September 2001, Europe Transport Policy for 2010', COM(2001)370 final.

48 COM(2011)827 final, 1 December 2011, Proposal for a Regulation of the European Parliament and the Council on Common Rules for the Allocation of Slots at European Union Airports (Recast).

49 See articles in *The Guardian*, 20 April 2015 and in *The Financial Times*, 15 February 2016.

50 Krishna R. Urs, US Deputy Assistant Secretary for Transportation, 'What Comes Next for US International Aviation Policy After 100 Liberalized Air Service Agreements?' Beijing, 25 May 2011, www.state.gov.e/eb/tra/rm/229214.htm, retrieved 24 February 2015.

51 *The Observer*, Business, 26 November 2006, 'Europe Accepts Its Role as the Green Pioneer of the World', p. 5.

52 European Commission White Paper, 'European Transport Policy for 2010: Time to Decide', COM(2001)370, 2001, p. 21.

53 International Panel on Climate Change, 'Summary for Policymakers',http://www. grida.no/climate/ipcc/aviation/index.htm.

54 *European Aviation Environmental Report 2016*, p. 13, www.ec.europa.eu, retrieved 20 September 2016.

55 *Ibid.*, p. 19.

56 US Department of State, Open Skies Partners, 2016, www.state.gov/e/eb/ris/othr/ ata/114805.htm, retrieved 20 September 2016.

57 These were the findings of a US Department of Transportation report: *International Aviation Developments, Second Report*, 'Transatlantic Deregulation: The Alliance Network Effect', US Department of Transportation, Office of the Secretary, October 2000.

58 Australian, New Zealand 2002 Aviation Agreement, http://www.aph.gov.au/binaries/house/committee/jsct/augustandseptember2002/report/chapt6.pdf, retrieved 23 February 2015.

59 *International Aviation Developments, Second Report*, pp. 2–5.

60 *Loder Collection*, HE 9762.5, Argyris address to European Air Law Association: Seminar on Airline Mergers and Competition in the EC, 27 July 1990.

61 Sorensen Interview, 12 September 2001.

62 US Department of Transportation and the European Commission, Transatlantic Airline Alliances: Competitive Issues and Regulatory Approaches, 16 November 2010, http://ec.europa.eu/competition/sectors/transport/reports/joint_alliance_report.pdf, retrieved 23 February 2015.

63 *Ibid.*, pp. 12–13.

64 *Ibid.*, p. 23.

65 V. Bilotkach and K. Huschelrath, 'Airline Alliances, Antitrust Immunity and Market Foreclosure', *Review of Economics and Statistics* 95(iv), (2013), pp. 1368–1383.

66 US Department of Transportation Bureau of Transportation Statistics, 2013 US Carriers, www.rite.dot.gov/bts/press_releases/bts012_14, retrieved 19 February 2015.

67 Much of this section is based on interviews conducted by the author and his friend and colleague Joe McKinney of Baylor University on 11 and 12 March 2008 with Paul Gretch, US Department of Transportation; Will Ris, Vice President for Government Affairs, American Airlines; Rebecca Cox, Vice President for Government Affairs, Continental Airlines; and Jeffrey Shane, recently retired from the US Department of Transportation.

68 See COM(2002)649, Final, 'Communication from the Commission on the consequences of the Court judgements of 5 November for the European air transport policy', 19 November 2002; and Commission versus Austria etc. European Court of Justice cases C-466/98 to C-476/98.

69 The Brattle Group, *Economic Impact of an EU-US Open Aviation Area*, www.Brattle.com/_documents/Publications/ArticleReport2198.pdf, retrieved 10 March 2007. I would like to acknowledge a debt to one of my postgraduate students, John Ruthven, for much of the narrative and analysis of the Brattle Group Report.

70 Cox interview 11 March 2008.

71 Senator Stevens also reportedly held a grudge against the Department of Transportation for its earlier approval of a merger between DHL and Deutsche Post over his strong opposition.

72 *The Observer*, 'BA Buys Up Heathrow Slots', 21 April 2002.

73 For detailed explanation of this see: Statement of Jeffrey N. Shane, Under Secretary of Transportation for Policy, Department of Transportation before the Subcommittee on Aviation and Commerce, Science, and Transportation, 9 May 2006.

74 US Department of Transportation and the European Commission, Transatlantic Airline Alliances: Competitive Issues and Regulatory Approaches, 16 November 2010, http://ec.europa.eu/competition/sectors/transport/reports/joint_alliance_report.pdf, retrieved 23 February 2015.

7 Conclusion
Unfinished business?

> *While there is indeed a trend pointing towards liberalization in the aviation sector, its history does not necessarily suggest a bandwagon effect tending towards free competition.*[1]

The end game for international civil aviation in a truly globalized industry does not necessarily have to be in the shape of free competition, though almost certainly from a pragmatic and practical point of view a high level of competition would most likely be present. As argued before, the essential feature, which defines a truly globalized market, is a level playing field with all actors playing the same game. In a theoretical sense where the balance is struck between regulation and competition is irrelevant. So where is the industry now in 2017 and how globalized has it become?

In the non-commercial field (though it is important to remember that there is no clear division between commercial and non-commercial), there have been huge strides forward since 1944. The ICAO, through its Council, Air Navigation Commission and Assembly, has been the central player. ICAO SARPS have established uniform, or in some cases minimum, standards and practices. In the last two decades it has taken important steps in oversight and implementation responsibilities in attempts to ensure that agreed standards are actually implemented. The level of smooth, safe and secure inter-operability that has been achieved between airlines, and airlines and national air navigation authorities, and airlines and airports and governmental authorities throughout the world is largely due to ICAO. However, IATA has also played a significant role, often in collaboration with ICAO. Both collate and publish important data for the industry, promote its profile and often take the lead in tackling challenges that arise for the airlines, such as the response to hijacking and terrorism. IATA has facilitated interlining and fare setting and other areas of economic cooperation between airlines. Its work has often been beneficial, but regarding fare coordination its work in the minds of liberals became dysfunctional and that role has now been much reduced. It would be possible to provide a plethora of statistics, systematic and anecdotal evidence of the success that ICAO and IATA have had over the years, but it is not really necessary. Two facts speak adequately of what they have achieved: the impressive safety of airline travel and the huge numbers of people who fly (relatively) efficiently and (usually) on time each year.

In 2014 in aircraft capable of carrying more than 14 passengers and excluding military aircraft and incidents involving military action, the global airline industry suffered 688 fatalities out of a total of approximately 3.1 billion passengers carried. In comparison about the same number of people die in the US every week as a result of car accidents. The statistical chances of dying in a passenger aircraft and through a shark attack are, respectively: 1:11 million and 1:1.3 million. According to one eminent statistician 'a traveler could on average fly once a day for 4 million years before succumbing to a fatal crash.'[2] And according at least to US and UK statistics they could expect to fly on time about 75% of the time.[3] The story in the sphere of safety, security, navigation and technical standards is one of steady incremental improvement with a body of rules, conventions and regulations emerging in the shape of ICAO SARPS and international law resulting in a growing uniformity for the industry. As always, the story is far more complex with less uniformity in the politically charged commercial sphere.

The main dynamics for change, over the last 70 years, have arisen from US policies and latterly specifically from its Open-skies policy and the market forces that those policies have helped to unleash. The US has helped deliver to the world a more effective, efficient, seamless and competitive commercial system that better serves the interests of consumers. Its policies have also helped foster other initiatives, most notably the SEAM, highly liberal agreements such as the EU-Canadian and the Australian-New Zealand aviation agreements, both of which go beyond Open-skies, and the ASEAN SAM, though that falls somewhat short of what one might expect from its name. What emerges overall is a definite movement towards more liberal practices and a progressive and incremental levelling of the playing field. However, two major players still resist Open-skies with other significant players, namely Russia and China. In both the power of the state looms large and, as with the case of the airlines from the UAE, questions arise about state aid and subsidies. With the spread of liberalization, state aids and subsidies have diminished hugely and those airlines embraced by the new dispensation are understandably hostile to 'competitors' in privileged positions because of persisting state aids and subsidies. In addition to problems raised by Russia, China and the general problem of state aids and subsidies, there also persist significant differences among the liberalized systems, which mean continuing imbalances in the competitive playing field. The international aviation industry is far from being uniform in its commercial practices and it is not easy to identify how best to proceed from where the industry now finds itself.

The EU, US and the ASEAN, and the prospects for a fully globalized international civil aviation market

The make-up of US Open-skies policy has been discussed and explained at length, but although inferred it has not been explicitly stated what it does *not* include. Now is the time to do that in order to assess fully its differences with the position adopted by the EU Commission. In 2011 Krishna Urs summarized what US Open-skies does not do. It does not allow foreign entry into US cabotage; US

Open-skies agreements do not authorize that 'in any form'. That still applies to scheduled services, though the US-Canadian Open-skies agreement of 2012 granted limited cabotage to charter services.[4] Traditional ownership and control remains in place. It does not guarantee provision of scarce slots, but does require non-discrimination under the original Bermuda principle of 'fair and equal opportunity'. 'Finally, an open skies agreement does not exempt one side's airlines from the requirement to comply with safety and security, and other requirements set by the other side.'[5]

Urs took pains to emphasize that any changes in the rules of ownership and control would 'of course . . . require action by Congress', which was simple code for saying it would not happen. Just in case anyone had not received the message though, later in the same speech, talking of an ICAO proposal for a Multilateral Convention on Foreign Investment in Airlines, he commented: 'it could open up opportunities for significant foreign investment in airlines if their authorities wish to allow it – *but it would not require the U.S. or any other country to change ownership and control rules for their own airlines*' [emphasis added].[6] US ambitions for the future are simply: more Open-skies agreements, preferably on a regional agreement basis, and ensuring that gains made are not lost through barriers such as scarce slots and environmental challenges. That seems rather modest compared with the stated ambitions of the European Commission.

In 2005 the European Commission drew up proposals which constituted a road-map for future developments both internally and externally. The external policy was structured round three pillars. The first was to seek legal certainty after the Court decision in 2002 about Community carriers and their incompatibility with bilateral national ASAs. The second was to extend the common aviation area beyond the EU, the European Economic Area (EEA: Norway, Liechtenstein and Iceland) and Switzerland, which already participate in the Single Market. And the third was to seek comprehensive agreements with key partners. All three pillars had achieved notable successes by 2012 when the Commission again reviewed matters. The legal position had been largely stabilized, most notably with the EU-US agreement of 2007. Expansion to neighbors included the West Balkans, Moldova, Georgia, Morocco and Jordan. And there were comprehensive agreements with key players, namely the US, Canada and Brazil. The 2012 policy statement, however, went on to identify what the Commission now saw as the major obstacle to further progress:

> Despite the progress made worldwide towards a more liberal regime for international air transport, governments have still not reformed the archaic ownership and control rules for airlines. Most countries still maintain rules stipulating that airlines be majority owned and controlled by their own nationals thereby denying carriers access to a wider range of investors and capital markets. The effect has been to impose an artificial industry structure on the airline sector that does not exist in other industries. Despite aviation's global reach, there is not a single truly global airline in the way that other industries have global companies.[7]

The Commission described alliances as 'the nearest proxy to global airlines' that we have, but clearly thought the industry could do better and that involved discarding cabotage and national ownership and control laws. The Commission was firm in its views: 'we have not made sufficient headway in tackling ownership and control restrictions. These threaten to ossify the development of a global industry.'[8] There is a major difference of view and emphasis here between the US and the EU. The former rests on the *de facto* situation, the existence of US cabotage and national ownership and control laws, and works from there to explore further liberalization through its Open-skies policy. The motives for that are complex and contentious. One reading of the American position is that a combination of security and commercial considerations dictates that ownership and control laws should not be changed because they would compromise US security and erode the market share currently held by US airlines. And different US officials put different weightings on the importance of these two considerations. Another reading is that while at least some US officials would be willing to change cabotage and ownership and control, they recognize that it is not politically possible because of views in the Congress, which are set by security and commercial considerations, some clearly traditionally protectionist. Whatever the case may be, and it is actually a complex amalgam of all these positions, the bottom line is that the US looks unlikely to take the last major step remaining towards a fully globalized airline industry. The EU is not; it does not accept that cabotage and ownership and control laws are here to stay.

Of agreements made by other countries only those by Canada with the EU and the Australian-New Zealand agreement approach the liberalism of what is now promoted by the EU. Both agreements have begun to erode cabotage and dilute national ownership and control laws. There has been significant liberalization elsewhere and it is important to register that increasingly power is shifting to the Middle East and Asia, where reform is taking place alongside important aviation countries where progress is less notable. Key players here are China and the ASEAN, Turkey and the UAE. In terms of ranking by passengers carried by a country's airlines, China is second, Indonesia eighth, Turkey ninth and the UAE twelfth. In addition to Indonesia's airlines, the ASEAN has a rapidly growing civil aviation sector elsewhere, such as in Malaysia and Singapore, and rather like the EU the ASEAN has embarked upon a route leading to a SAM to help generate more efficiency and a better deal for consumers. However, its story is not fully compatible with Europe's.

There are not the same legal drivers arising from supranational integration and the emphasis in the ASEAN is on the concepts of consensus and compromise, as it is in the EU, but because the framework in the ASEAN is nowhere near as solid as in Europe, there have to be broader and more flexible concepts of both. As one study puts it: 'many of the agreements within ASEAN provided a technical opt-out clause for members, creating leeway to the community policy. The ASEAN system was designed to facilitate collaboration and consensus building, not confrontation or enforcement.'[9] Even so, there have been major developments within the ASEAN and it is instructive for an overview of the global situation to examine how the changes came about.

The ASEAN was in fact something of a latecomer to aviation liberalization, partly because of government ownership of airlines, which had similar effects to the protectionist conservatism that arose from the same source in Europe. There was also the financial crisis, which hit the region in 1997 and cast everything into disarray. Ironically, Thailand, which sparked the crisis, was in 2000 the first to deregulate its domestic airline industry. Indonesia and others followed and in a pattern familiar on the transatlantic, the infection spread, with several dynamics eventually impacting on international operations, in particular the appearance of new low-cost carriers. As economies throughout most of Asia achieved extraordinary rates of economic growth, the demand for air travel burgeoned and helped to promote liberalization. In 2003 Singapore followed the Thai example, but with a difference as its airline industry was exclusively international. The domestic deregulation movement in the ASEAN had already spawned domestic low-cost operators, but Singapore now created Valuair and Tigerair to compete exclusively in the international field. Singapore unsurprisingly signed Open-skies agreements with Indonesia and Brunei in 2004. So, there were clearly similarities with developments between the US and Europe, but there were also significant differences.

The movement towards a single market was more hesitant than in Europe and took place in a less supportive context because ASEAN does not have the same degree of political integration. A milestone was the establishment of a roadmap for reform, which has over the years borne fruit.[10] In 2009 the ASEAN introduced Third and Fourth Freedoms for capital cities, but both Indonesia and the Philippines opted out. A year later Indonesia, Brunei, Cambodia and Laos also opted out of the step to full Open-skies liberalization: the Philippines acceded, but with restrictions maintained on access to Manila. The granting of cabotage rights and Seventh Freedoms are not currently on the agenda and ownership and control are simply at present a bridge too far. There are also significant differences among the ASEAN on external relations. The ASEAN signed an Open-skies policy with China in 2010, but the Philippines and Indonesia opted out: Thailand already had an Open-skies agreement with China signed in 2004. From all this emerges a more liberal regime for the ASEAN, but one that has within it a mosaic of differences of a kind that do not apply in the SEAM. As one authority put it in May 2016 after the ASEAN SAM finally came into effect:

> The implementation of this policy has met several hurdles, including significant reluctance from Indonesia and the Philippines, and is unlikely to be fully carried out until after 2016. Despite these impediments, the Open Skies policy should gradually increase policy convergence and liberalization among ASEAN member states and boost the region's connectivity.[11]

Final thoughts

Currently there does not exist a single fully globalized component in the international airline industry: but, it is hugely successful and has moved steadily towards a more globalized condition. The greatest successes have been in technical, safety, navigational, security and weather forecasting for airline operations. Where politics does not inject national political preferences, or where it is relatively easy to achieve a political consensus when they do, then standardization, uniform practices and governance have moved forward. Where politics has intruded then serious challenges have been posed. Some have been overcome, with only few and minor caveats (for example virtual universal acceptance of Freedoms 1 and 2),[12] but others, particularly in the commercial field, have not.

However, even in the commercial field, successes are legion and in particular regarding liberal route access, liberal capacity and frequency, and market pricing: the three inter-connected conditions identified in the COMPAS Report for a more efficient market. In addition state aids and subsidies have diminished hugely, though they have still not been entirely exorcized from the industry and levels vary even among the states with liberal operating policies. The larger problems that persist are cabotage and national ownership and control, which are now the two main remaining obstacles for further development of a truly globalized industry. As the EU Commission has put it, these regulations threaten to ossify the industry in its present mold. European liberals had hoped that the EU-US aviation agreement would have abandoned ownership and control and cabotage, thus creating an Open Aviation Area between the US and the EU, which would have had sufficient critical mass gradually to draw in the rest of the world. That did not happen because of US reservations about its wisdom and that has left the world wondering what major development can come next. Without US participation regarding the abandonment of ownership and control and cabotage, it is doubtful that any major progress worldwide can be made except in terms of the US's long-standing policy of Open-skies. There is room for improvement by continuing to deploy that strategy, but it cannot deliver a truly globalized international civil aviation system.

***

The 1920s witnessed remarkable individual achievements in the air, best epitomized by Charles Lindberg's solo non-stop flight in the Spirit of St Louis across the Atlantic in May 1927, but that decade also blazed the way for the commercialization and advancement of civil aviation in the 1930s. In 1929 the Dornier DO-X made a record that was to hold for many years by carrying 150 passengers, a crew of 10 and nine stowaways in a demonstration flight. It was generally intended to carry 100 passengers or 66 passengers for long-haul flights. While something of a phenomenon, plagued by mishap and technical problems, the DO-X was never a commercial success. By way of contrast, in October 1929, the Handley Page Hannibal Class HP42, capable of carrying a more modest number of 38 passengers (in the HP42W version), began operations, but over the following 15 years it carried 100,000 passengers without a single fatal accident.[13] Civil aviation was indeed taking off in the 1920s and 1930s, but it was not just as a result of matters upon which this study has primarily focused: machines, pilots, commercial airlines, governments and international institutions both NGO and inter-governmental. People – the potential consumers – also needed to awaken to the possibilities of flight and not just flight for the *élite*. How that awakening occurred and how attitudes towards air travel developed in the collective mind of air travelers – apart from a few brief observations – is beyond the scope of this study, but aviation enthusiasts and aviation journals played a crucial part. In the first editorial of *Popular Flying* in July 1932, the editor embarked upon a mission to accomplish the awakening of minds to the attraction of flying. *Popular Flying* was an important publication and by 1934 it had the greatest circulation of any aviation magazine in the world: close on 25,000 copies a month. The editor argued:

> *Popular Flying* will leave no stone unturned to banish the notions, which have done so much to retard the progress of civil aviation, notions which confine aviation to a chosen few, either wealthy, or possessed of a physique beyond ordinary standards. . . . Individually, sooner or later, everybody will fly, because it is the quickest, easiest and most pleasant from of transport yet discovered.[14]

In the twenty-first century such restrictive notions have long been banished with customers ranging from new-born babies to the very elderly and from all walks of life, some with only the most modest of incomes, taking to the air. Airlines and the industry have indeed travelled a long way from their international infancy in the 1930s and even from the 1940s when British and US airlines were restricted to two transatlantic round-trip flights a week each, but the journey is not yet complete. It goes on and one suspects that the balance between regulation and liberalization will continue to shift and change in response to technological changes, market opportunities, environmental and security issues and, while politics abides in the industry, in response to government policies. In this sense the future will not be radically different from the past. One can no longer say 'politics is all', but international civil aviation is still tied to politics. Over the years, and especially since the 1944 Chicago Conference, the Gordian knot has been loosened, but never been untied. It is doubtful if it will be in the foreseeable future. Indeed in the current economic and political world climate, a tightening seems as likely as a further loosening.

Notes

1 Jeremy Chua and Matthew Ramsey, 'The Heavens Were Not Free: Towards Airline Deregulation & Multilateral Open Skies in the U.S., EU, & ASEAN Cases', http://www.helvidius.org/wp-content/uploads/2014/06/Airline-Deregulation.pdf, retrieved 25 February 2015.
2 www.ICAO.int/Newsroom/News%20Doc%202013/COM.43.13.ECON-RESULTS. Final-2.en.pdf, retrieved 27 February 2015; www.aviation-safety.net, retrieved 27 February 2015; T. Barrabi, 'Despite Germanwings Flight 4U9525 Crash, Odds of Dying in

a Plane Crash Are Low', www.ibtimes.com, retrieved 23 January 2017, citing statistician A. Barnett of the MIT.

3 www.transtats.bts.gov US figures for 2014, 75.28% of flights were on time; www.caa.org.uk 75% of UK flights in third quarter 2014 were on time: both retrieved 27 February 2015.

4 US officials are apt to caution that what it does with Canada is a special case and should not be taken as a precedent for urging similar action elsewhere.

5 Urs, *What Comes Next for US International Aviation Policy*.

6 *Ibid.*

7 COM(2012)556 final, Communication from the Commission to the European Parliament, the Council, the European Economic and Social Committee and the Committee of the Regions: The EU's External Aviation Policy – Addressing Future Challenges, 27 September 2012. The Council adopted it in December 2012.

8 COM(2012)556 final, p. 4.

9 Jeremy Chua and Matthew Ramsey, 'The Heavens Were Not Free: Towards Airline Deregulation & Multilateral Open Skies in the U.S., EU, & ASEAN Cases', http://www.helvidius.org/wp-content/uploads/2014/06/Airline-Deregulation.pdf.

10 ASEAN, *ASEAN Transport Action Plan 2005–2010*, http://www.asean.org/news/item/asean-transport- action-plan-2005–2010.htm, retrieved 26 February 2015.

11 'The State of ASEAN Aviation in 2016', ASEAN Briefing 6 May 2016, www.ASEAN briefing.com, retrieved 20 September 2016.

12 One such exception has been a long-running dispute between the EU and Russia over over-flight charges levied until 2014 by Aeroflot on non-stop flights from Europe across Siberia to Asia. Estimates vary, but cost is about $200 million per year. As of 2014 the charge is paid to the Russian authorities.

13 Information for this is taken from Alan P. Dobson, *FDR and Civil Aviation: Flying Strong, Flying Free*, London and New York: Palgrave/Macmillan, 2011; William H. Longyard, *Who's Who in Aviation History*, Shrewsbury: Airlife Publishing Ltd. 1994; *The Guinness Book of Aircraft: Records, Facts and Feats*, London: Guinness Publishing Limited, 1988.

14 Johns, editorial *Popular Flying*, vol. I(i), 1932; see also Alan P. Dobson, 'Captain W.E. Johns and Biggles: Aviation; Travel; and Fighting Aloft', in José Domingues, Dominique Faria, António Monteiro, Fátima Outeirinho (editors), *Écrivains-aviateurs, Aviateurs-écrivains*, Paris, Éditions Le Manuscrit, forthcoming.

References

Books

Allison, G.T., *Essence of Decision: Explaining the Cuban Missile Crisis*, Boston: Little Brown, 1971

Armitage, M.J. and R.A. Mason, *Air Power in the Nuclear Age, 1954–84: Theory and Practice*, Basingstoke: Macmillan, 1985

Bailey, G.J., *The Arsenal of Democracy: Aircraft Supply and the Anglo-American Alliance 1938–1942*, Edinburgh: Edinburgh University Press, 2013

Baldwin, D.A., *Neorealism and Neoliberalism: The Contemporary Debate*, New York: Columbia University Press, 1993

Banner, S., *Who Owns the Sky? The Struggle to Control Airspace from the Wright Brothers On*, Cambridge: Harvard University Press, 2008

Bednarek, J.R.D., *America's Airports: Airfield Developments, 1918–1947*, College Station: Texas A&M University Press, 2001

Bender, M. and S. Altschul, *The Chosen Instrument: Pan Am, Juan Trippe, the Rise and Fall of an American Entrepreneur*, New York: Simon and Schuster, 1982

Berle, B.B. and T.B. Jacobs (editors), *Navigating the Rapids 1918–71: From the Papers of A.A. Berle*, New York: Brace Jovanovich, 1973

Branker, J.W.S., *IATA and What It Does*, Leyden: Sitjhoff, 1977

Bull, H., *The Anarchical Society: A Study of Order in World Politics*, New York: Columbia University Press, 1977

Button, K., K. Haynes and R. Stough., *Flying Into the Future: Air Transport Policy in the European Union*, Cheltenham: Edward Elgar, 1998

Chuang, R.Y., *The International Air Transport Association*, Leiden: Sijthoff, 1972

Colegrove, K.W., *International Control of Aviation*, Boston: World Peace Foundation, 1930

Cross, J.A., *Sir Samuel Hoare: A Political Biography*, London: Jonathan Cape, 1977

Daley, R., *An American Saga: Juan Trippe and His Pan Am Empire*, New York: Random House, 1980

Diederiks-Verschoor, I.H.Ph. (revised by Pablo Mendes de Leon), *An Introduction to Air Law*, 9th edition, The Netherlands: Kluwer Law International, 2012

Dienel, H-L. and P. Lyth (editors), *Flying the Flag: European Commercial Air Transport Since 1945*, Basingstoke: Macmillan, 1998

Dobson, A.P., *Peaceful Air Warfare: The United States, Britain, and the Politics of International Aviation*, Oxford: Clarendon Press, 1991

Dobson, A.P., *Anglo-American Relations in the Twentieth Century: Of Friendship, Conflict, and the Rise and Decline of Superpowers*, London: Routledge, 1995

Dobson, A.P., *Flying in the Face of Competition: The Policies and Diplomacy of Airline Regulatory Reform in Britain, the USA and the European Community 1968–94*, Aldershot: Avebury Press, 1995

Dobson, A.P., *Globalization and Regional Integration: The Origins, Development and Impact of the Single European Aviation Market*, London, Routledge, 2007

Dobson, A.P., *FDR and Civil Aviation: Flying Strong, Flying Free*, New York: Palgrave Macmillan, 2011

Doganis, R., *Flying Off Course: The Economics of International Airlines*, London: Allen and Unwin, 1985

Douhet, G., *The Command of the Air*, New York: Arno Press, 1942

Erdmenger, J., *The European Transport Policy*, Aldershot: Gower, 1983

Gialloreto, L., *Strategic Airline Management: The Global War Begins*, London: Pitman Press, 1988

Giemulla, E.M. and L. Weber (editors), *International and EU Aviation Law: Selected Issues*, The Netherlands: Kluwer Law International, 2013

Greenwood, J., *Interest Representation in the European Union*, Basingstoke: Palgrave, 2003

Haanappel, P.P.C. and G. Petsikas (editors), *EEC Air Transport Policy and Regulation and Their Implications for North America*, Deventer: Kluwer, 1989

Haas, E.B., *Beyond the Nation State: Functionalism and International Organization*, Stanford: Stanford University Press, 1964

Havel, B.F., *Beyond Open Skies: A New Regime for International Aviation*, The Netherlands: Kluwer International Law, 2009

Hoffmann, S., *The State of War: Essays on the Theory and Practice of International Politics*, New York: Praeger, 1965

Holgrefe, J.L. and R. O. Keohane (editors), *Humanitarian Intervention: Ethical, Legal, and Political Dilemmas*, Cambridge: Cambridge University Press, 2003

Hollis, M. and S. Smith, *Explaining and Understanding International Relations*, Oxford: Clarendon Press, 1991

Hugill, P.J., *World Trade Since 1431*, Baltimore and London: John Hopkins University Press, 1993

Jönsson, C., *International Aviation and the Politics of Regime Change*, London: Frances Pinter, 1987

Keohane, R.O., *After Hegemony: Cooperation and Discord in the World Political Economy*, Princeton: Princeton University Press, 1984

Keohane, R.O. and J. S. Nye, *Power and Interdependence*, Boston: Little Brown, 1977

Keynes, J.M., *The Economic Consequences of the Peace*, London: Macmillan, 1920

Kimball, W.F., *Churchill and Roosevelt: The Complete Correspondence, 3 volumes*, London: Collins, 1984

Krasner S.D. (editor), *International Regimes*, Ithaca: Cornell University Press, 1983

Lewis, C., *Sagittarius Rising*, Barnsley: Frontline Books, 2009, first published 1936

Lundestad, G. (editor), *No End to Alliance: The United States and Western Europe, Past, Present and Future*, Basingstoke & New York: Macmillan & St. Martin's, 1998

Lycklama á Nijeholt, J. F., *Air Sovereignty*, The Hague: Martinus Nijhoff, 1910

Mackenzie, D., *ICAO: A History of the International Civil Aviation Organization*, Toronto: Toronto University Press, 2010

Majone, G. (editor), *Deregulation or Re-Regulation? Regulatory Reform in Europe and the United States*, London and New York: Pinter and St. Martins, 1990

McGowan, F. and C. Trengove, *European Aviation: A Common Market?* London: Institute for Fiscal Studies, 1986

Milward, A., *The European Rescue of the Nation State*, 2nd edition, London: Routledge, 1999

Mitrany, D., *A Working Peace System: An Argument for the Functionalist Development of International Organization*, London: Royal Institute for International Affairs, 1943

Oakeshott, M., 'On the Activity of Being A Historian', in Michael Oakeshott, *Rationalism in Politics and Other Essays*, Indianapolis: Liberty Press, 1991, pp. 137–168

Oduntan, G., *Sovereignty and Jurisdiction in the Airspace and Outer Space: Legal Criteria*, Abingdon: Routledge, 2012

Peterson, B.S., *Bluestreak: Inside Jetblue, the Upstart that Rocked the Industry*, New York: Portfolio, 2004

Pinder, J., *Altiero Spinelli and the British Federalists: Writings by Beveridge, Robbins and Spinelli, 1937–43*, London: Federal Trust, 1998

Pisano, D.M., *To Fill the Skies with Pilots: The Civilian Pilot Training Program 1939–1949*, Urbana: University of Illinois Press, 1993

Pryke, R., *Competition Among International Airlines*, Aldershot: Gower, 1987

Reynolds, C., *Theory and Explanation in International Relations*, London: Martin Robertson, 1973

Ruston, R., *A Say in the End of the World: Morals and British Nuclear Policy 1941–1987*, Oxford: Oxford University Press, 1990

Sampson, A., *Empires of the Sky: The Politics, Contests and Cartels of World Airlines*, London: Hodder and Staughton, 1984

Sandholtz, W. and A.S. Sweet (editors), *European Integration and Supranational Governance*, Oxford: Oxford University Press, 1998

Serling, R. J., *When the Airlines Went to War*, New York: Kensington Books, 1997

Shaw, S., *Airlines and Management*, London: Pitman, 1985

Solberg, C., *Conquest of the Skies: A History of Commercial Aviation in America*, Boston: Little Brown and Co., 1979

Stadlmeier, S., *International Commercial Aviation: from Foreign Policy to Trade in Services*, Paris: Edition Frontiers, 1998

Stevens, H., *Liberalisation of Air Transport in Europe: A Case Study in European Integration*, London: European Institute, LSE, 1997

Stevens, H., *Transport Policy in the European Union*, Basingstoke: Palgrave, 2004

Walker, J.S., *Henry A. Wallace and American Foreign Policy*, Westport: Greenwood Press, 1976

Wassenbergh, H.A. and H.P. van Fenema (editors), *International Air Transport: A Legal Analysis*, Deventer: Kluwer, 1981

Wells, H.G., *The War in the Air*, London: Gollanz, 2011

Wheatcroft, S. and G. Lipman, *Air Transport in a Competitive European Market: Problems, Prospects and Strategies*, London: Economist Intelligence Unit, Economist Publications Ltd., 1986

Wilbur R.L. and H.M. Hyde, *The Hoover Policies*, New York: Scribner's, 1937

Woodward, E.L. and R. Butler (editors), *Documents on British Foreign Policy 2nd Series vol. 4*, London: HMSO, 1950

Articles and chapters in edited collections

Bilotkach, V. and K. Huschelrath, 'Airline Alliances, Antitrust Immunity and Market Foreclosure', *Review of Economics and Statistics*, 95(iv), (2013) 1368–83

Breyer, S.G., 'Working on the Staff of Senator Ted Kennedy', *Legislation and Public Policy* 14, (2011), 607–10

Cooper, J.C., 'Some Historic Phases in British International Civil Aviation Policy', *International Affairs*, 23, (1947) 189–202

Devereux, D.R., 'State Versus Private Ownership: The Conservative Governments and British Civil Aviation 1951–62', *Albion*, 27(i), (1995) 65–85

Devereux, D.R., 'British Planning for Postwar Civil Aviation 1942–1945: A Study in Anglo-American Rivalry', *Twentieth Century British History*, 2(i), (1991) 26–46

Dobson, A.P., 'Regulation or Competition: Negotiating the Anglo-American Air Services Agreement of 1977', *The Journal of Transport History*, 15, (1994) 144–65

Dobson, A.P., 'Flying Between Britain and the USA: Canadian Civil Aviation 1935–1945', *International History Review*, 34(4), (2012) 655–77

Dobson, A. P., 'Not the Third World War: The US-UK Heathrow Succession Rights Affair and Anglo-American Relations', *Diplomacy and Statecraft*, 25(iii), (2014) 529–49

Dobson, A.P., 'Captain W.E. Johns and Biggles: Aviation; Travel; and Fighting Aloft' in J. Domingues, D. Faria, A. Monteiro, F. Outeirinho (editors), *Écrivains-aviateurs, Aviateurs-écrivains*, Paris, Éditions Le Manuscrit, forthcoming

Dobson, A.P. and J. Mckinney, 'Sovereignty, Politics and US International Airline Policy', *Journal of Air Law and Commerce*, 74(iii), (2009) 527–53

Feldstein, M., 'The Retreat from Keynesian Economics', *The Public Interest*, (Summer 1981) 92–105

Forsyth, P., 'Airline Deregulation in the United States: The Lessons for Europe', *Fiscal Studies*, 4, (November 1983) 7–21

Garland, G., 'The American Deregulation Experience and the Use of Article 90 to Expedite EEC Air Transport Liberalisation', *European Competition Law Review*, 7, (1986) 193–4

Gormly, J.L., 'The Counter Iron Curtain: Crafting an American-Soviet Bloc Civil Aviation Policy 1943–1960', *Diplomatic History* 37(1), (2013) 248–79

Haas, E.B. 'Why Collaborate? Issue-Linkage and International Regimes', *World Politics* 32, (1980) 357–405

Hershey, A.S., 'The International Law of Aerial Space', *The American Journal of International Law*, 6(ii), (1912) 381–8

ICAO Journal (2014) 'Air Transport Development: Setting the Course', *ICAO Journal*, 69(iii), (2014) 33–37

Macbrayne, S.F., 'The Right of Innocent Passage', *McGill Law Journal*, I, (1954–55) 271–83

Moravcsik, A., 'Preferences and Power in the European Community: A Liberal Intergovernmentalist Approach', *Journal of Common Market Studies*, 31(iv), (1993) 473–524

Nayar, B.R., 'Regimes, Power, and International Aviation', *International Organization*, 49(i), (1995) 139–71

Scott-Smith, G., and D. J. Snyder, 'A Test of Sentiments: Civil Aviation Politics and the KLM Challenge in Dutch-American Relations', *Diplomatic History*, 37(v), (2013) 917–45

Sochor, E., 'International Civil Aviation and the Third World: How Fair Is the System?', *Third World Quarterly*,10(iii), (1988) 1300–22

Warner, E., 'ICAO after Four Years', *Air Affairs*, 3(2), (1950) 281–97

Primary sources

Act of Incorporation, Articles of Association, Rules and Regulations, IATA 9th Publication: Montreal, IATA, 1967

Assess: Assessment of the contribution to TEN and other transport measures to the mid-term implementation of the White paper on European Transport Policy for 2010, Transport and Mobility Leuven, 28 October 2005 for DG TREN

British Government Command Paper 9218, *Civil Aerial Transport Committee Report*, 12 December 1918

British Government Command Paper 266, *Convention Relating to International Air Transport*, 1919

British Government Command Paper 1739, *First Report on the Imperial Air Mail Service*, 1922

British Government Command Paper, Cmd. 6747, *US, UK, Civil Air Services Agreement Bermuda*, 1946, Bermuda Final Act

British Government Command Paper, Cm 8584, *Aviation Policy Framework*, March 2013

British National Archives, London, CAB Papers

Canadian National Archives, Ottawa

Papers of W.L. Mackenzie King

MG 26 J4

RG70

Papers of C.D. Howe

Coopers and Lybrand, *Application and Possible Modification of Council Regulation 95/93 on Common Rules for the Allocation of Slots at Community Airports*, 17 October 1995

EC Bulletin

EC Regulations, European Press Releases and other official papers including for example:

White Paper 'Completing the Internal Market', COM(85)310, May 1985

'Civil Aviation Memorandum 2: Progress Towards the Development of a Community Air Transport Policy', COM(84)72, Final, 15 March 1984

Report from the Commission to the European Parliament and the Council on the Implementation of the Single Sky Legislation: Time to Deliver', COM(2011)731 final, 14 November 2011

Case 167/73, Commission v. France, 1974 ECR, 359

European Commission Directorate-General Energy and Transport, *Single European Sky: Report of the high-level group*, Brussels, November 2000

Expanding Horizons: A report by the Comité des Sages for Air Transport to the European Commission, January 1994

Franklin D. Roosevelt Library, Hyde Park, New York, FDR Official File

PSF

Rowe Papers

Berle Papers

Hopkins Papers

Foreign Relations of the United States (FRUS), various volumes Washington DC, US Government Printing Office, printed from time to time

International Air Transportation Competition Act of 1979, US PL 96–192, 15 February 1980

International Aviation Developments, Second Report, 'Transatlantic Deregulation: the Alliance Network Effect', US Department of Transportation, Office of the Secretary, October 2000

Jimmy Carter Presidential Library, Atlanta, Georgia

Loder Collection, Swansea University Library (including much official EC papers and letters and copies of the *Official Journal*)

Official Journal of the European Community

Report of the Committee on Transport of the European Parliament on Memorandum 2 of the Commission, the *Klinkenborg Report*, PE Doc A2–86/85/A, 7 August 1985

Report on Competition in Intra-European Air Services, 1982, Paris, ECAC, CEAC Doc. No. 25, the COMPAS Report

The Rome Treaty

Smithsonian National Aeronautical and Space Museum Archives, Washington DC, Trippe
Papers

Staff Offices, Domestic Policy Staff

US Federal Register

UK House of Lords Record Office London, Beaverbrook Papers

US National Archives, Washington DC,
State Department Decimal Files
RG 197 CAB
WHCF

Web sources

'2013 ICAO Air Transport Results Confirm Robust Passenger Demand, Sluggish Cargo
Market', International Civil Aviation Organization, www.ICAO.int/Newsroom/
News%20Doc%202013/COM.43.13.ECON-RESULTS.Final-2.en.pdf

'Air transport, passengers carried', The World Bank, http://data.worldbank.org/indicator/
IS.AIR.PSGR

'Agreement between the Government of Australia and the Government of New Zealand relating to Air Services, Parliament of Australia, www.aph.gov.au/binaries/house/committee/
jsct/augustandseptember2002/report/chapt6.pdf

ASEAN Briefing, www.ASEANbriefing.com

Aviation Safety Network, www.aviation-safety.net

Bureau of Transportation Statistics, United States Department of Transportation, www.
transtats.bts.gov

Chua, J. J., and M. Ramsey, 'The Heavens Were Not Free: Towards Airline Deregulation
and Multilateral Open Skies in the U.S., EU, and ASEAN Cases', Columbia University, Journal of Politics and Society, Web Feature, 12 June 2014, www.helvidius.org/
wp-content/uploads/2014/06/Airline-Deregulation.pdf

Civil Aviation Authority (UK), www.caa.co.uk

Civil Aviation Authority (London), www.caa.org.uk

Edinburgh Airport, www.edinburghairport.com

European Commission, www.ec.europa.eu

International Air Transport Association (IATA), www.IATA.org

IATA website, Operational Safety Audit

www.iata.org/pressroom/facts_figures/fact_sheets/Pages/ses.aspx

www.iata.org/publications/Pages/wats.aspx

'Transatlantic Airline Alliances: Competitive Issues and Regulatory Approaches, European
Commission and the United States Department of Transportation', 16 November 2010,
http://ec.europa.eu/competition/sectors/transport/reports/joint_alliance_report.pdf

'UK – US transatlantic air traffic down 3.3% in 2010; British Airways add-
ing winter capacity on existing routes', Anna Aero, www.anna.aero/2011/01/19/
uk-us-transatlantic-air-traffic-down-3pc-in-2010/

US Government State Department and Department of Transportation websites

'What Comes Next for U.S. International Aviation Policy After 100 Liberalized Air Services Agreements?', U.S. Department of State, https://2009-2017.state.gov/e/eb/tra/
rm/229214.htm

www.eurocontrol.int/ses/public/standard_page/sk_ses.html

www.state.gov/e/eb/ris/othr/ata/114805.htm

www.rite.dot.gov/bts/press_releases/bts012_14
www.Brattle.com/_documents/Publications/ArticleReport2198.pdf
www.asean.org/news/item/asean-transport- action-plan-2005–2010.htm

Interviews by the author

Dell, Edmund, UK Secretary of State for Trade 1976–78, London, 8 December 1989
Ebdon, Robert, Head of Government Affairs, British Airways, 5 August 1991
Fennes, R., DGVII, Brussels, 21 February 2000
Murphy, Cyril, Vice President for International Affairs, United Airlines, United Airlines Headquarters Chicago, 1 July 1991
Pogue, Welch, CAB Chairman 1942–1946, 1 August 2000 at the Cosmos Club Washington DC
Shane, Jeffrey N., Assistant Secretary for Policy and International Affairs, US Department of Transportation, Department of Transportation Washington DC, 5 April 1991
Sorensen, F., DGVII, Brussels, 21 February 2000
Sorensen, F., DGVII, Brussels, 12 September 2001
Interviews conducted by Joe McKinney of Baylor University and the author on 11 and 12 March 2008 in Washington DC with Paul Gretch, US Department of Transportation; Will Ris, Vice President for Government Affairs American Airlines; Rebecca Cox, Vice President for Government Affairs Continental Airlines; and Jeffrey Shane recently retired from the US Department of Transportation.

Confidential interviews by the author

Senior official from the UK CAA, London, 23 May 2001
Senior official DG IV, Brussels, 22 February 2000
Interview: official from DG IV, Brussels, 22 May 1991
Interviews with three Commission officials 1 from DG TREN (previously DG7), and two officials from the DG for Competition (formally DG4), both conducted 25 September 2006

Ephemera

Aerospace International
Financial Times
Flight International
The Guardian
The Independent
New York Times
The Observer
The Times
Speech by Jeffrey N. Shane, Assistant Secretary for Policy and International Affairs, US Department of Transportation, 'Air Transport Liberalization: Ideal and Ordeal', Royal Aeronautical Society, Montreal, 8 December 2005.
Remarks by Jeffrey N. Shane, Under Secretary for Policy, US Department of Transportation, International Aviation Club, Washington DC, 12 September 2006

New York Post

'European Airline Traffic after 1993', presentation by F. Sorensen, VII.C.1–839/90, 8 April 1991

Remarks by Lord King, Royal Aeronautical Society 125th Anniversary Banquet, 16 May 1991

Richard Branson, Address to the IEA Conference, 6 October 1993

Neumeister speech 'Better Use of Airport Slots in the EU', Düsseldorf, Hochtief AirPort Symposium, 17 September 2001

Index

For Product Safety Concerns and Information please contact our EU
representative GPSR@taylorandfrancis.com Taylor & Francis Verlag GmbH,
Kaufingerstraße 24, 80331 München, Germany

Printed and bound by CPI Group (UK) Ltd, Croydon, CR0 4YY

01/05/2025

01858401-0001